Library Technology
REPORTS
Expert Guides to Library Systems and Services

The Current and Evolving Landscape of Bibliometric Tools and Technologies

Laura Bredahl

ALA TechSource
American Library Association

Library Technology
REPORTS

ALA TechSource purchases fund advocacy, awareness, and accreditation programs for library professionals worldwide.

Volume 58, Number 8

The Current and Evolving Landscape of Bibliometric Tools and Technologies

ISBN: 978-0-8389-3792-1

DOI: https://doi.org/10.5860/ltr.58n8

American Library Association

225 N. Michigan Ave., Suite 1300
Chicago, IL 60601-7616 USA
alatechsource.org
800-545-2433, ext. 4299
312-944-6780
312-280-5275 (fax)

Editor

Samantha Kundert

Copy Editor

Judith Lauber

Production

ALA Production Services

Cover Design

Alejandra Diaz and ALA Production Services

Library Technology Reports (ISSN 0024-2586) is published eight times a year (January, March, April, June, July, September, October, and December) by American Library Association, 225 N. Michigan Ave., Suite 1300, Chicago, IL 60601-7616. It is managed by ALA TechSource, a unit of the publishing department of ALA. Periodical postage paid at Chicago, Illinois, and at additional mailing offices. POSTMASTER: Send address changes to Library Technology Reports, 225 N. Michigan Ave., Suite 1300, Chicago, IL 60601-7616.

ALA TechSource

About the Author

Laura Bredahl is the bibliometrics and research impact librarian at the University of Waterloo where she currently supports university leadership, faculties, departments, and the broader community in research impact and bibliometric analyses, services, use, and governance. She supports strategic planning and decision making, grant proposals, and celebrating research excellence at all levels within the university. Previously, she was a STEM liaison librarian with the Davis Centre Library, at the University of Waterloo. Bredahl is an active member in the bibliometric community in North America and is currently a deputy blog editor with *The Bibliomagician*, an internationally known blog that deals with topics related to bibliometrics. She serves on the ORCID-CA Governing Committee, a group that provides governance and operational oversight to a Canada-wide consortium of ORCID members administered through the Canadian Research Knowledge Network. She has presented on bibliometric topics at CNI, OCLC, SciVal North American User Group, and the Bibliometrics and Research Impact Community Conference.

Abstract

While bibliometrics has been around for decades, with the recent development of new bibliometric tools, there has been a surge in interest in bibliometric services at academic institutions in North America. Navigating this rapidly evolving landscape can be a challenge for academic institutions as they attempt to determine which tools and skill sets will best meet their needs. This issue of *Library Technology Reports*, "The Current and Evolving Landscape of Bibliometric Tools and Technologies" (vol. 58, no. 8), will help guide decision makers and practitioners in their selection and use of current bibliometric tools and related systems, and it will offer some insight into future directions.

Contents

Chapter 1

Introduction to Bibliometrics and Current Data Sources

What Is Bibliometrics?

A Very Short History

The term *bibliometrics* is widely attributed to Alan Pritchard from his 1969 paper titled "Statistical Bibliography or Bibliometrics" (Andrés 2009; Gingras 2016; Pritchard 1969). However, before the term was coined, bibliometrics was already emerging as a viable scientific discipline in the 1960s, in large part due to the foundation of the Institute for Scientific Information (ISI) led by Eugene Garfield and the subsequent development of the Science Citation Index (SCI; Mokhnacheva and Tsvetkova 2020). The intention in creating the SCI was to "eliminate the uncritical citation of fraudulent, incomplete, or obsolete data by making [scholars] aware of criticisms of earlier papers" (Garfield 1955). Later, the ISI recognized the power of the data available in the SCI for creating networks among journals and their citations and developed what is now the widely used (and disputed) Journal Impact Factor (JIF), the average citations per publication. The JIF rose in popularity at Garfield's suggestion that it would be helpful to librarians for managing library collections. However, less discussed in the literature are Garfield's other suggested applications, which include use by individual researchers for selecting reading lists, by editors for evaluating journal performance, and in the study of science policy and research evaluation (Garfield 1972). Although there have been mounting critiques on the limitations of the JIF, many of these described applications remain core to bibliometrics more broadly, even though the JIF may not be the metric of choice.

Defining Bibliometrics

Despite the continually evolving methods of analysis, the heart of bibliometrics remains the counting of documents, their related bibliographic information, and their network of citations. The rise and widespread adoption of bibliometrics have relied on the development of computer-based indexes and databases that enable the capture of the necessary bibliographic metadata and allow that metadata to be stored, linked, searched, shared, and ultimately analyzed using mathematical methods.

What Is Bibliometric Data? Bibliographic Metadata as the Input to Bibliometrics

As suggested by the history and definition of bibliometrics, the core of bibliometric data is based on the bibliographic metadata available about a wide range of document types. Today, bibliometric data largely relies on indexing and citation databases that capture an ever-expanding and robust set of bibliographic metadata and are therefore also constrained by it. Table 1.1 lists the most common bibliographic metadata that underpins most bibliometric calculations. There is often confusion between what is considered bibliographic data and what is considered bibliometric data. Although there is certainly overlap, data transitions from bibliographic data into bibliometrics when it is aggregated, counted, or used in some mathematical formula. In other words, bibliographic data is the input, and bibliometrics is the output.

Something should also be said about the types of documents that are included in bibliometric analysis. Since bibliometrics is dependent on the databases that capture the needed data, the types of publications available in these databases dictate what can be included. Typically, indexing and citation databases (such as Web of Science, Scopus, etc.) include these publication types: journal articles, review articles, conference proceedings papers, books, book chapters, editorials, and letters. Some also capture errata, corrections, and preprints. However, there are also an increasing number of new document types being

Table 1.1: Bibliographic metadata used in bibliometrics

Bibliographic Metadata Types	Metadata Fields
Document	Document title Journal/book/source title Publication year Volume/issue Page numbers ISSN/ISBN Document level identifiers (DOI, PMID, ArxivID, etc.) Publication type Source type Language Open access status
Author	Author names Author identifiers Affiliation name Affiliation address Affiliation country
Content	Abstract Author keywords Indexed keywords Journal level classifications Article level classifications
Citation	Reference list Document level citation count
Funding	Funding body name Funding body address

captured, including data papers and short surveys.[1] The set of publication types is ever-expanding as institutions and researchers recognize the biases in bibliometrics when it focuses on only a discrete set of publication types.

More generally, almost any metadata field that is supplied about a document has the potential to be added into a bibliographic data set; therefore, bibliometric systems or tools are continually adding to the complexity of the available data.

What Are the Major Sources of Bibliometric Data?

There are surprisingly few data sources of bibliographic metadata that include the full suite of data required to perform robust bibliometrics. The challenge lies in providing extensive citation linking between the source document, reference lists, and those that cite it. This exponentially expands the size of the data set and poses an insurmountable challenge (or at least a pretty large challenge) for many bibliographic databases. The network (or citation mapping, as it is often called) created through this linking is the fundamental power of the data sources used for bibliometric analysis.

To date, only a few bibliometric sources provide citation linking within their bibliographic data. These include the following (Visser, van Eck, and Waltman 2021):

- **Web of Science:** Owned by Clarivate Analytics, Web of Science is a very large multidisciplinary database that is made up of several indices to which an institution can subscribe selectively. These indices are made up of a curated list of journals and publications that are reviewed against quality standards for inclusion. Although the subject areas covered are still heavily focused on the sciences, Web of Science continues to grow its coverage of social sciences, arts, and humanities.
- **Scopus:** Owned by Elsevier, Scopus is a very large multidisciplinary database that is largely made up of a curated list of journals and publications, which are reviewed against quality standards for inclusion. The subject areas covered are still heavily focused on the sciences, with approximately 27 percent (as of April 2022) of its content on the social sciences (which include arts, humanities, business, economics, decision sciences, and psychology; Scopus 2022).
- **Dimensions:** Owned by Digital Science, Dimensions is a very large multidisciplinary database that ingests metadata from freely available online sources such as Crossref, PubMed, and PubMed Central and then supplements the database with licensed content directly from publishers. The Dimensions platform is also a bibliometric assessment tool, making it different from Web of Science and Scopus, which offer primarily the bibliographic source data with limited analytical tools. Dimensions also provides some free access to its system and noncommercial access to its data via API.
- **Crossref:** Owned by Publishers International Linking Association, Crossref is a not-for-profit metadata service that allows its members—made up of publishers, institutions, funding agencies, and government agencies—to register their content and mint DOIs for the purposes of reference linking. It provides free access to their metadata and encourages ingest into external systems for wide use.
- **OpenAlex:** As a response to Microsoft Academic pulling the plug in late 2021 (a huge blow to open-source systems engineers; Singh Chawla 2021; Microsoft 2021), the nonprofit company OurResearch developed OpenAlex. It adheres to its open-source principles making its index of research entities—such as scholarly papers, authors, and institutions—available openly on its web application via API and an entire local database download snapshot for offline access.

There is a difference between the bibliographic sources listed above and the bibliometric tools used to analyze the data. This section focuses on the sources of bibliographic data that feed into the bibliometric tools that will be further explored in chapter 2. However, for many of these data sources and bibliometric tools, the lines are becoming blurred as more data sources are integrated into existing systems and as new companies emerge and form new innovative tools and integrate existing ones.

There is also a growing number of systems that provide robust bibliometric data but are not considered sources of bibliometric data because they are not primarily used to feed into external systems for additional analysis. Systems such as Lens.org (Cambia), the Leiden Ranking (Centre for Science and Technology Studies), and Scite.ai use external data sources, then supplement the data with in-house reference linking intended to enhance their citation analysis capabilities.

Although many bibliometric tools are available, nearly all draw on at least one of the bibliographic sources Web of Science, Scopus, Crossref, or OpenAlex (and previously Microsoft Academic). However, the distinction between the data sources for bibliometric systems is further blurred as new, highly intelligent multipurpose systems emerge, such as Scite.ai, Lens .org, and Bibliometrix (see chapter 2 for even more systems), that integrate ever-expanding types of data sources. Bibliometric tools no longer simply produce bibliometrics based on citation linking between scholarly documents such as journal articles, conference proceedings, or books. They now provide metadata on grants, patents, clinical trials, research data sets, policy documents, and more. An increasing number of tools are linking this complex data together from across content types to provide more complete profiling opportunities at the institution, department, and researcher levels. For example, many of the tools link patents and articles to provide a count of articles that have received patent citations (see chapter 3 for a use case). These articles can then be analyzed by a number of factors, such as research areas, top author, coauthorship, geographic distribution, and so on.

Google Scholar has yet to be mentioned. This is primarily due to its virtual lack of usefulness as a data source. Google Scholar provides a massive searchable database of scholarly materials, including citation linking and citation counts that often outnumber other systems; however, it does not allow the data to be easily exported to other systems or linked to from other systems for use, thereby disqualifying it as a practical bibliometric data source. With that said, Harzing's Publish or Perish (PoP) does pull Google Scholar data into its system (using an API access token) and offers a number of citation indicators. Still, PoP has to deal with the annoying issue of Google Scholar sending CAPTCHAs when the PoP system sends queries at too high a rate, just to make sure there is an actual person using the PoP and it is not just a massive data harvester (Harzing.com 2022). This roadblock is likely why every other system out there does not attempt to ingest Google Scholar data.

What Are Bibliometric Indicators?

Bibliometric indicators are the output of bibliometrics built from bibliographic metadata. Indicators make visible otherwise invisible phenomena. Bibliometrics is intended to answer questions about research productivity, impact, excellence, collaboration, networks, and more. However, these phenomena are largely unobservable unless proxies are used to represent them. Therefore, observable measures—such as counts of authors, documents, citations, affiliation, and so on—are used to represent the unobservable phenomena to be examined (Sugimoto and Larivière 2018). Cassidy Sugimoto and Vincent Larivière, as well as Yves Gingras (Gingras 2016), offer excellent further reading on the validity of indicators, which is beyond the scope of this report.

Bibliometric indicators are typically divided into several groups:

- **Productivity indicators** give insight into the activity of an entity,[2] measured through publication/document counts.
- **Impact indicators** give insight into the attention given to a document or set of documents of an entity, usually measured through citation counts, including citations in other research output, policy, clinical trials, knowledge syntheses, or patents.
- **Collaboration indicators** give insight into the amount of overlap between two entities and the nature of this overlap, usually measured by coauthorship and affiliation data.
- **Interdisciplinarity indicators** give insight into the overlap of research areas by looking at research outputs resulting in collaborations between authors from different disciplines or at research outputs citing or spanning more than one discipline.
- **Alternative metrics** are a growing set of indicators that may eventually evolve into separate standard categories on their own. However, this report groups them together not because of their newness but because the selections of indicators, their data sources, and the ways these indicators are grouped and presented are so different among the various bibliometric tools that it is difficult to describe with any consistency. However, in general, alternative metrics include the following indicators:
    - social media attention, measured through tweets, likes, blog post links, and so on
    - views and use, measured through database/

Table 1.2: Introductory bibliometric indicators

Productivity Indicators			
Metric	***Description***	***Variations***	***Caveats***
Number of documents	The total number of documents from a specific entity (e.g., country, institution, group, etc.).	Temporal analysis options are common (e.g., number of documents per year). The selection of publication types included will impact counts.	Avoid making comparisons across disciplines, author at different career stages, and entity size. Suggest using productivity alongside other normalizing indicators and/or with trend information. The data source determines the publications that are included.
Impact Indicators			
Metric	***Description***	***Variations***	***Caveats***
Number of citations	Total number of citations received from a subset of documents (e.g., country, institution, group, etc.).	Include or exclude self-citations. Percent of the total number of documents.	Expected to trend downward toward most current years. Citations take time to accumulate. Avoid making comparisons across disciplines, author at different career stages, and entity size.
Number of documents cited	Total number of documents that have received at least 1 citation.	Include or exclude self-citations. Percent of the total number of documents.	Avoid making comparisons across disciplines, author at different career stages, and entity size.
Number of citations per paper	Total number of citations divided by the number of documents within an entity (e.g., country, institution, group, etc.).	Include or exclude self-citations.	Expected to trend downward toward most current years. Citations take time to accumulate. Avoid making comparisons across disciplines, author at different career stages, and entity size.
Number of documents in the top-most cited documents worldwide	Calculates the total number of documents from an entity (e.g., country, institution, group, etc.) that are in the top percentages of all cited documents.	Most often available as top 1%, 10%. Percent of the total number of documents. Can be field- or subject-weighted. Temporal analysis options are common. Include or exclude self-citations.	Can be a relatively small number causing large variances in trend data.
Normalized citation impact	Normalization usually occurs by discipline/subject/field, publication year, and publication type. The normalized value is then compared to an expected normalized global value, and the metric is represented as an index relative to 1 that indicates the expected global value.	Include or exclude self-citations. Journal normalization uses the journal the document is published in for normalization rather than the subject, year, and publication type.	Small entities, such as individual authors or small groups, will see large variances in trend data.
Collaboration Indicators			
Metric	***Description***	***Variations***	***Caveats***
Number of documents with coauthor at another institution	Total number of documents with co-authors at another institution or entity type.	Percent of the total number of documents. Corporate or industry/academic co-authorship. National/domestic coauthorship. International coauthorship. Institutional coauthorship.	Collaboration practices vary among disciplines, institution type, and geographic regions.

Table 1.3: Why leaders should care about responsible metrics

Arguments	Description
Maintain institutional autonomy	Take control of what is actually being measured to align with your institution's values, as opposed to being reactive to external evaluations.
Make better decisions	Ensure that what you intend to evaluate is really being measured, aligning the indicators with the phenomena of interest. Make sure bibliometrics is truly needed for the evaluation, and include other, qualitative approaches.
Ensure return on investment	Ask whether the bibliometrics approach is the best way, and if it is, ensure that there is sufficient investment to pursue meaningful evaluation.
Establish operational readiness	Understand what responsible research evaluation policies and external expectations exist or are in development.
Manage reputational risk and enhance staff well-being	Get ahead of poorly used metrics, especially where they impact individual reputations and well-being. Too much attention to metrics begets too much attention to metrics. Balance in the evaluation and assessment should include a compassionate approach to the impact on scholars' work and life.

Source: Adapted from the INORMS Research Evaluation Group documentation. For full descriptions, see INORMS Research Evaluation Group 2020a.

reference manager clicks, downloads, and saves
- media attention, measured through news media coverage
- recommendations, measured through post-publication peer review

There is a wide variety of bibliometric indicators, too many to provide a comprehensive overview here. However, table 1.2 provides an overview of the main indicators commonly presented in bibliometric assessment tools. These are largely descriptive analyses, which must be distinguished from more rigorous statistical analyses. Ana Andrés's book *Measuring Academic Research: How to Undertake a Bibliometric Study* provides excellent in-depth guidance on selecting specific indicators to apply to a bibliometric research study (Andrés 2009). However, for more detail, see chapter 3 of this report, which will provide some guidance on general applications of bibliometric indicators.

The indicators presented in table 1.2 are derived in large part from the bibliometric tools SciVal (Elsevier 2019), Incites (Clarivate 2022), Dimensions (Dimensions 2021), and Lens.org (Lens.org 2022). These tools are pervasive within the global bibliometric community and provide a bridge between bibliometric practitioners, who typically provide bibliometric services to their institutions and academic staff with an entry or intermediate level of experience with bibliometrics, and expert-level bibliometric services or researchers, who conduct more advanced calculations and methodologies that require data science or statistical knowledge (Lancho Barrantes, Vanhaverbeke, and Dobre 2021; Cox et al. 2019). This is an important distinction, as bibliometrics is a complex historied field, and practitioners (often librarians within academia) can feel adrift when faced with the mathematical complexities of the statistical analyses presented in bibliometric research papers. In addition to these tools, the University of Waterloo's white paper "Measuring Research Output through Bibliometrics" was also used as a guiding information source (Byl et al. 2016).

Responsible Use of Metrics

A highly effective bibliometric practitioner is . . . value-led, not data-led.

—Gadd 2020

It is essential that bibliometrics be approached with a duty to responsible use. This becomes particularly salient when working with individuals holding decision-making power at all levels throughout academia. The INORMS Research Evaluation Group (2020a) outlines several reasons senior leaders should be interested in responsible evaluation of research, which include maintaining institutional autonomy, making better decisions, ensuring return on investment, establishing operational readiness, and managing reputational risk and enhancing staff well-being (table 1.3). The work coming out of INORMS is crucial for a bibliometric practitioner to understand. Its work is a response to the vast amount of professional experience of its members and integrates learnings from the impacts of the UK Research Evaluation Framework and leading internationally recognized statements of principles such as the Leiden Manifesto (Hicks et al. 2015), the San Francisco Declaration of Research Assessment (DORA 2012), and the Metric Tide report (Wilsdon et al. 2015; see also table 1.4). Therefore, the resulting INORM *SCOPE Framework* (INORMS Research Evaluation Group 2020b) is intended to be a bridge between the ideals stated in these principles and the business of doing bibliometrics.

SCOPE is an acronym for Start, Context, Options, Probe, and Evaluate, and the *SCOPE Framework* is

Table 1.4: Snapshot of responsible use of metrics declarations, manifestos, and principles

	Milestones	**Audience**	**Key Messages**
DORA—"San Francisco Declaration on Research Assessment" (DORA 2012)	established 2012 22,162 signatories as of Sept. 2022	funding agencies institutions publishers metrics suppliers researchers	Eliminate journal-based metrics that mask the merits of individual works (aka dump the JIF). Release online publications from the confines of print.
The Metric Tide report (Wilsdon et al. 2015)	released 2015 revisited 2022	anyone conducting quantitative evaluations of research particularly relevant to the UK Research Excellence Framework environment	Set of five principles for the use of any metrics. Considers robustness, humility, transparency, diversity, and reflexivity in the use of any quantitative indicators.
"The Leiden Manifesto" (Hicks et al. 2015)	released 2015	administrators practitioners researchers	Set of 10 principles for the use of bibliometrics. Quantitative evaluations should not supplant qualitative ones. If they are used, however, they should be situated appropriately within the context of the researcher, the institution, the region, and the field. Transparency is key.
INORMS SCOPE Framework (INORMS Research Evaluation Group 2020a)	released 2021	anyone conducting evaluations of research	Start with value. Make evaluations context-specific. Consider the validity of the methods. Probe deeper into latent consequences. Evaluate the evaluations.

meant to guide the practitioner through a series of steps that help with adherence to responsible use of metric principles. These steps walk through fundamental questions helping the practitioner to first question the reasons for using metrics, match the level of analysis to the need, identify appropriate methodologies, dig deeper into the potential and known effects of the analysis, and finally evaluate whether the goals of the analysis were achieved. Following these steps is practical, and beyond setting up any bibliometric project with sound judgments, they can also be used as a communication tool for establishing standard expectations for research evaluation within institutions.

Notes

1. These are new document types from Scopus (Elsevier 2020): data papers are short descriptive papers about data sets; errata report errors, corrections, and retractions of published papers; and short surveys are short (only a few pages) reviews of research.
2. Entities can represent a person, group, institution, region, etc., and can be subdivided by subject, discipline, years, etc.

References

Andrés, Ana. 2009. *Measuring Academic Research: How to Undertake a Bibliometric Study.* Amsterdam, The Netherlands: Elsevier.

Byl, Lauren, Jana Carson, Annamaria Feltracco, Susie Gooch, Shannon Gordon, Tim Kenyon, Bruce Muirhead, et al. 2016. "Measuring Research Outputs through Bibliometrics." Working paper. January 2016. https://doi.org/10.13140/RG.2.1.3302.5680.

Clarivate. 2022. "Normalized Indicators." InCites Help. Accessed September 22. https://incites.help.clarivate.com/Content/Indicators-Handbook/ih-normalized-indicators.htm.

Cox, Andrew, Elizabeth Gadd, Sabrina Petersohn, and Laura Sbaffi. 2019. "Competencies for Bibliometrics." *Journal of Librarianship and Information Science* 51, no. 3: 746–62. https://doi.org/10.1177/0961000617728111.

Dimensions. 2021. "Which Indicators Are Used in Dimensions, and How Can These Be Viewed?" Last modified September 19. https://dimensions.freshdesk.com/support/solutions/articles/23000018839-which-indicators-are-used-in-dimensions-and-how-can-these-be-viewed-.

DORA. 2012. "San Francisco Declaration on Research Assessment." December 15, 2012. https://sfdora.org/read/.

Elsevier. 2019. *Research Metrics Guidebook*. https://elsevier.widen.net/s/chpzk57rqk/acad_rl_elsevierresearchmetricsbook_web.

Elsevier. 2020. *Scopus Content Coverage Guide*. https://www.elsevier.com/__data/assets/pdf_file/0007/69451/Scopus_ContentCoverage_Guide_WEB.pdf.

Gadd, Elizabeth. 2020. "The Five Habits of Highly Effective Bibliometric Practitioners." Keynote address, Bibliometrics and Research Assessment Symposium 2020, online, October 7–9. National Institutes of Health Library. YouTube video, 58:01. https://youtu.be/SFi1NbbSdQ8.

Garfield, Eugene. 1955. "Citation Indexes for Science: A New Dimension in Documentation through Association of Ideas." *Science* 122, no. 3159: 108–11.

———. 1972. "Citation Analysis as a Tool in Journal Evaluation." *Science* 178, no. 4060: 471–79. https://doi.org/10.1126/science.178.4060.471.

Gingras, Yves. 2016. *Bibliometrics and Research Evaluation: Uses and Abuses*. Cambridge, MA: MIT Press.

Harzing.com. 2022. "Why Do You Give Me These Stupid CAPTCHAs?" Frequently Asked Questions, last updated June 2. https://harzing.com/resources/publish-or-perish/manual/about/faq#004.

Hicks, Diana, Paul Wouters, Ludo Waltman, Sarah de Rijcke, and Ismael Rafols. 2015. "Bibliometrics: The Leiden Manifesto for Research Metrics." *Nature* 520, no. 7548: 429–31. https://doi.org/10.1038/520429a.

INORMS Research Evaluation Group. 2020a. "Five Arguments to Persuade HE Leaders to Evaluate Research Responsibility." https://inorms.net/wp-content/uploads/2020/06/five-ways-to-persuade-leaders-to-evaluate-responsibly.pdf.

INORMS Research Evaluation Group. 2020b. *The SCOPE Framework: A Five-Stage Process for Evaluating Research Responsibly.* INORMS Research Evaluation Group. https://inorms.net/wp-content/uploads/2021/11/21655-scope-guide-v9-1636013361_cc-by.pdf.

Lancho Barrantes, Barbara S., Hannalore Vanhaverbeke, and Silvia Dobre. 2021. "2021 Competency Model for Bibliometric Work." *Bibliomagician* (blog). https://thebibliomagician.wordpress.com/competencies/.

Lens.org. 2022. "Glossary." Support. Accessed September 22. https://support.lens.org/glossary/.

Microsoft. 2021. "Next Steps for Microsoft Academic—Expanding into New Horizons." *Microsoft Academic* (blog), May 4. https://www.microsoft.com/en-us/research/project/academic/articles/microsoft-academic-to-expand-horizons-with-community-driven-approach/.

Mokhnacheva, Yu. V., and V. A. Tsvetkova. 2020. "Development of Bibliometrics as a Scientific Field." *Scientific and Technical Information Processing* 47, no. 3: 158–63. https://doi.org/10.3103/S014768822003003X.

Pritchard, A. 1969. "Statistical Bibliography or Bibliometrics?" *Journal of Documentation* 25, no. 4: 348–49.

Scopus. 2022. "Scopus Sources List." https://www.scopus.com/sources.

Singh Chawla, Dalmeet. 2021. "Microsoft Academic Graph Is Being Discontinued. What's Next?" News, Nature Index. June 15. https://www.nature.com/nature-index/news-blog/microsoft-academic-graph-discontinued-whats-next.

Sugimoto, Cassidy R, and Vincent Larivière. 2018. *Measuring Research: What Everyone Needs to Know.* Oxford: Oxford University Press.

Visser, Martijn, Nees Jan van Eck, and Ludo Waltman. 2021. "Large-Scale Comparison of Bibliographic Data Sources: Scopus, Web of Science, Dimensions, Crossref, and Microsoft Academic." *Quantitative Science Studies* 2, no. 1: 20–41. https://doi.org/10.1162/qss_a_00112.

Wilsdon, James, Liz Allen, Eleonora Belfiore, Philip Campbell, Stephen Curry, Steven Hill, Richard Jones, et al. 2015. *The Metric Tide: Report of the Independent Review of the Role of Metrics in Research Assessment and Management.* https://doi.org/10.13140/RG.2.1.4929.1363.

Chapter 2

Bibliometric Tools for Academia

What Are Bibliometric Tools? And How Do Bibliometric Tools Differ from Research Discovery Tools?

Bibliometric tools, at their core, integrate the data available from bibliographic data sources (as discussed in chapter 1) and make the data available in the form of bibliometric indicators. There are a variety of standard and proprietary bibliometric indicators that vary among the available tools, which will be discussed with some further detail in this chapter. We must be careful not to confuse the limited bibliographic data sources with the almost countless bibliometric tools or technologies available today. Many bibliographic data sources will provide some very limited bibliometrics, such as some basic descriptive analysis based on the number of publications, authors, and so on, while others provide slightly more robust bibliometrics, such as results sets analysis, views of author profiles that contain bibliometrics, and views of some institutional level metrics (see table 2.1). Still, these are not often considered bibliometric tools because their main function is not to provide bibliometric analyses, but rather research discovery.

Yet it is difficult to precisely define how bibliometric tools differ from the typical research discovery tool since linking bibliographic data together is at the core of both. However, bibliometric tools provide richer data sets and analysis functions that

- rely on more complex mapping of the bibliographic data, particularly the citation data;
- aggregate or summarize this data into bibliometric indicators;
- allow for in-system visualizations and saving of data sets for additional analysis outside the system; and
- use data at a scale that requires significantly more computer processing power to provide this data.

Table 2.1: Bibliographic Sources with analytical views

Product Name	Owner/Developer
Scopus	Elsevier (RELX)
Web of Science	Clarivate

Bibliometric tools can be divided by the types of analysis that they attempt to perform, with two major classifications:

1. Descriptive bibliometric analysis tools summarize data and indicators such as total publications over time, citation counts, author counts, and other more complex computations of indicators.
2. Descriptive network analyses (often referred to as knowledge mapping or knowledge graphs) compute and visualize connections between bibliographic variables such as authors, keywords, affiliations, and so on.

Most practitioners of bibliometrics will engage with additional tools to help with the analysis and visualization of the bibliometrics outside of their system of choice, such as Excel, SQL, R, Python, Jupyter, GYPHY, Pajek, Tableau, Power BI, and so on. When going beyond the descriptive bibliometrics and network analysis, some researchers and practitioners will also employ statistical analysis tools such as SPSS, Excel Analysis ToolPak, SAS, or R. These ancillary tools are beyond the scope of this report.

Current Bibliometric Tools and Their Features

This section reviews the current bibliometric tools available, including descriptive bibliometric analysis tools and bibliometric and network analysis tools. Also discussed is the recent explosion of discovery tools that employ analytical views and network analysis.

Descriptive Bibliometric Analysis Tools: The Major Commercial Players

Table 2.2: Entity type comparisons across major commercial bibliometric tools

	InCites	*SciVal*	*Dimensions*	*Lens.org*
Entity Types Available for Analysis				
Publication sets	yes	yes	yes	yes
Authors (individual)	yes	yes	yes	yes
Custom author groups	no	yes	no	no
Institutions	yes	yes	yes	yes
Geographic regions	yes	yes	yes	yes
Journal-level research categories	yes	yes	yes	yes
Article-level research categories	yes	yes	yes	yes
Source titles	yes	yes	yes	yes
Funding bodies	yes	yes	yes	yes
Patents	no	no	yes	yes

InCites, SciVal, Dimensions, and Lens.org are the current major commercial bibliometric tools available that provide web-based applications with in-system analysis in a relatively user-friendly manner that does not require any coding or data-cleaning knowledge. These systems are ideal for the bibliometric practitioner who wants a relatively broad range of descriptive statistics about research outputs and impact. InCites, SciVal, and Dimensions are all subscription-based. Lens.org currently allows free access for noncommercial use to individuals and sells subscriptions to commercial users and institutions. Dimensions has a limited free view and enhanced subscription access. These systems stand out from other systems because they are aimed at generalist users and do not require any specific technical knowledge, such as application configurations or programming languages. However, the systems still use quite sophisticated analytical functions in the background and present them in their web-based applications.

These systems are aimed at a wide breadth of users including researchers, academic institutions, publishers, funders, and research and development departments of commercial enterprises.

SHARED FEATURES

- are web-based, intuitively structured applications with no downloading or local installations required
- allow the creation and analysis of aggregated bibliometric data that is based on the selection or creation of the various entity types available in the system (See table 2.2 for the types of entities available in these tools.)
- present data in tables or charts with download options (All allow CSV, among other options.)
- allow the saving of data in reports or dashboards within the web application
- offer user guides, tutorials, technical services, and substantial ongoing system development road maps

BASIC DATA STRUCTURES IN THESE SYSTEMS

InCites, Dimension, and Lens.org all work on a filtering basis, similar to the experience of searching within a research database (see figures 2.1, 2.2, and 2.3). This means that the system starts with the entire data universe available in the system and then allows the use of filters to narrow down the data set. For example, a user can specify an institution or institutions they plan to analyze and then filter by a subject category. This allows for significant flexibility within the system for analysis. The entity types listed in table 2.2 are used to view the created data set from the perspective of the selected entity type. Using this example, the data set for the specified institution and subject category could be analyzed by author, source titles, funding bodies, and so on.

SciVal begins analyses by creating and saving custom data sets that are then added to an entity staging area where they can be selected under different views that allow analyses such as benchmarking and trend analysis (see figure 2.4). Although SciVal allows for only a limited amount of filtering and customization of entities on the fly, its advantage is that multiple custom or preloaded data sets can be selected and benchmarked together.

Entity Types—The Key to Understanding the Features of These Major Bibliometric Tools

Table 2.2 presents an overview of the main entity types available for analysis in each of these major commercial bibliometric tools. Entity types are not the same as the content types (see table 2.3 on p. 17 for content types) as they integrate data from the various data sources associated with the content types to allow for analysis. For example, in InCites, the author entity type (called Researchers in InCites) can be analyzed in a variety of ways, including looking at the number of documents an author has published that have been cited by patents. However, because patents are not an entity type in InCites, patents themselves cannot be analyzed, and the data is therefore limited to the single patent-citation metric. On the other hand, both Dimensions and Lens.org have patent entity types that have a more robust set of data analyses and indicators associated with patents.

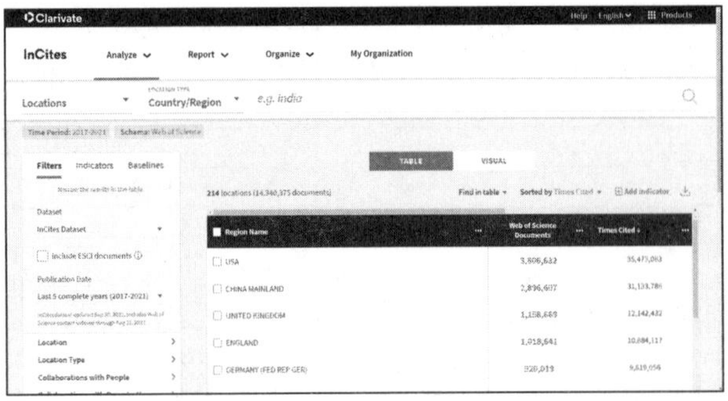

Figure 2.1
InCites interface with characteristic filtering on left-hand side of the screen. The Locations module is selected here; other options are Researchers, Organizations, Research Areas, Publication Sources, and Funding Agencies. No filters applied.

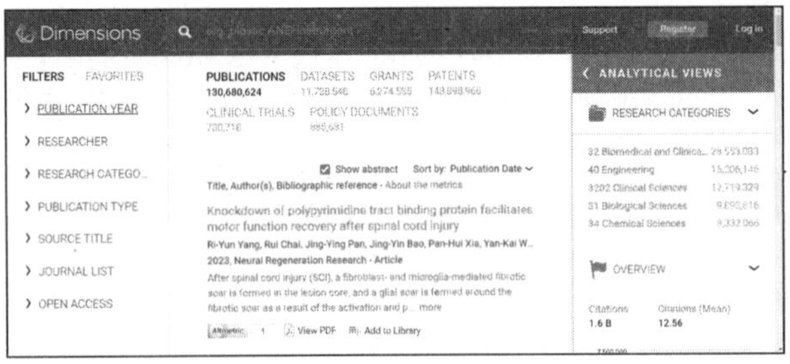

Figure 2.2
Dimensions interface with characteristic filtering on left-hand side of the screen. Publications is selected as the entity type; other entity types for analysis are Datasets, Grants, Patents, Clinical Trials, and Policy Documents. No filters applied.

PUBLICATION SETS

Publication sets are the core type of data set for any bibliometric system. They are highly customizable sets of documents and can be achieved through two main methods: (1) defined by search queries or other bibliographic metadata filters or (2) imported documents via direct connection from the data source or using persistent identifiers (e.g., DOIs). The specific steps to create, save, and analyze publication sets vary across these main bibliometric tools; however, they all use both methods to achieve these goals. In both SciVal and InCites, static publication sets can be created within the system using filters, by beginning with other data sets or from an export from the data source (i.e., Scopus for SciVal or WOS for InCites). Dimensions and Lens.org (and in a limited way SciVal using its Research Areas builder) achieve a similar goal by allowing researchers to save advanced Boolean search queries within the system. In this way these three bibliometric tools act as discovery tools as well. The advantage to this method is that the publication sets can be more dynamic, updating any time they are selected to run in the system, exactly like a saved search option available within many research databases. If you do not like this feature and need

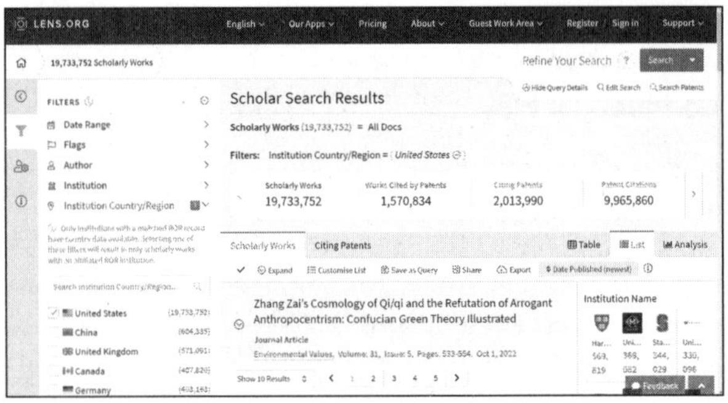

Figure 2.3
Lens.org interface with characteristic filtering on left-hand side of the screen. The Scholarly Works app is selected. There is also a Patents app available that allows similar search and analysis functions as the Scholarly Works app. A filter for United States publications is applied.

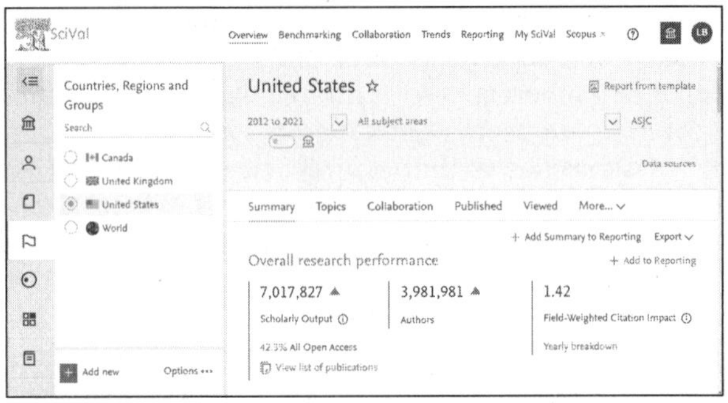

Figure 2.4
SciVal interface with characteristic entity staging area on left-hand side of the screen. The overview module is selected with the Countries, Regions and Groups entity type selected. The United States has been added to the staging area panel and selected. Data is filtered to the 2012–2021 publication years.

your publication sets to be a snapshot in time, Lens .org also provides the option for the search queries to be dynamic or static.

SciVal, InCites, and Lens.org allow publication sets to be bulk-uploaded using unique document identifiers, such as DOIs or system-assigned document numbers. These publication sets will always be static lists of publications but have the advantage of being highly customizable to the users' needs. These are usually managed under a tool that will save the files in folders within the system. It's not clear whether this same functionality is possible in Dimensions.

AUTHORS AND CUSTOM AUTHOR GROUPS

Authors, researchers, scholars—as they are variously called within these systems—present several challenges for analysis:

- author disambiguation,
- analysis of individual authors, and
- analysis of custom author groups.

Regarding disambiguation, all these systems use machine learning algorithms to help disambiguate authors and match them to documents within the systems. These algorithms usually take into account available metadata, such as name variants, existing author IDs (such as ORCID), affiliation data, research fields, journal names, common coauthors, and publication years. SciVal mints a unique identifier for each author, called the Scopus ID, and allows for merging and corrections when errors are found. InCites (as of 2022) has begun integrating its proprietary WOS Author Record into its Researchers filters within the system, and we can anticipate that researchers will be easier to disambiguate once these WOS Author Records reach full launch. Dimensions does not display a unique author ID minted by its system, but it integrates and displays ORCID and Scopus IDs and allows corrections to be requested from its customer service. Lens.org does not display a unique author ID minted by its system, but it will display an author's ORCID or Microsoft Academic ID if available.

All these systems allow individual authors to be analyzed and show up in author lists based on the selected bibliometrics within the system. They all have some type of author profile link as well that brings together the author's publications and usually lists affiliation, coauthors, and other simple bibliometrics that can be helpful to authors looking for their metrics or to verify an author's identity. InCites and SciVal link to author profiles outside of the bibliometric tool (i.e., to WOS or Scopus), while Dimensions and Lens.org contain the profiles within their systems.

Custom author groups refers to an in-system tool that allows the creation and management of author groups as a single entity that can be analyzed. Technically, a search could be conducted in any of these systems that combines all the required authors based on name or some unique author identifier (e.g., ORCID); however, SciVal is the only system that currently has an in-system tool for author and author group management that allows dynamic grouping, creation of hierarchies, and bulk editing of the group. Dimensions allows the selection of authors by using filters and stores the group in a workspace where groups can be edited or downloaded, but it does not allow hierarchies in the data structure. The custom author groups feature is of particular interest to the analyses of whole departments or specific research teams within an institution because of the customizability (see chapter 3 for an example). This type of analysis might also be achieved using a Current Research Information System, or CRIS; however, this report does not cover such systems in detail as they focus on institutional research information that displays and connects robust information about authors and the groups and research areas they belong to. In-depth bibliometric analysis is not the primary focus of these systems, although they do often display some indicators on the interface.

INSTITUTIONS

The analysis of whole institutions is ubiquitous within these systems, and over the last several years several of the bibliometric tools have improved the reliability of the institutional level data through either reviewing the accuracy of the affiliation names and hierarchies or through better integrating organizational unique identifiers such as the Research Organization Registry (ROR) and Ringgold ID. InCites (via WOS) and SciVal (via Scopus) recently underwent large reviews of their in-system institutional hierarchies to help validate and better capture affiliation data. Lens.org uses the ROR identifier to aid in disambiguating institutions. Dimensions links institutions with relational data but keeps each institution separated, outside of a hierarchy, to allow for more granular analyses.

GEOGRAPHIC REGIONS

Geographic regions are identified by the location of the affiliation. This is a standard, straightforward entity type across all these bibliometric tools. Therefore, there is not a lot of variation in how the names data is presented in these systems; most present country names and major regions like North America, Asia Pacific, and so on. A recent study by Guerrero-Bote et al. (2021) found that when aggregating data to the institution or country level, the Scopus data set maintained a larger count of documents/citations than did Dimensions, despite Dimensions having a greater total count of publications in its system. This illustrates that the completeness of the metadata fields impacts the filtering and data aggregation capacity of the system. Therefore, to aid in data validation and reporting, users should be familiar with the intricacies of their chosen tools.

Also, the types of indicators (i.e., publication counts, citations) available and the download options for visualizations, particularly geographic mapping, can vary greatly among these tools. Ideally, the data is downloadable from the data table and an image file is available from the system. This enables the user to either render a visualization external to the tool or take advantage of the images from the system. InCites appears to be the only system that allows proper image files (PNG, GIF, etc.) of visualizations to be downloaded. This is not an insurmountable challenge as the data tables can be used to create maps with external software, such as Tableau, Microsoft Power BI, R, or Leaflet, and a screen capture can create any needed image files. Users of geographic data usually want to be able to interact with the data but also want to add the maps to static reports; therefore, it is important to carefully consider how these bibliometric tools best meet a particular need. This is likely an area where we will continue to see improvements in these tools.

JOURNAL-LEVEL RESEARCH CATEGORIES

Journal-level research categories are research area classifications that have been assigned to a journal title, often referred to as a research area schema. There are many of these classifications. Some are specific to the bibliometric tool, such as the Web of Science Research Areas and the Scopus All Science Journal Classification (ASJC). However, there are many external schemata that have international or regional significance and have been mapped into the system using the existing classification structures. For example, the field of Research and Development, a classification scheme by the Organisation for Economic Co-operation and Development (OECD), is mapped to the Scopus ASJC. These types of mapping and use of classifications at the journal level allow for broad level analysis of knowledge domains. There are also critiques of these journal-level classifications. They tend to mask the true topic of a scholarly work by grouping all the works under the subject area of the journal. This is particularly problematic for multidisciplinary journals that cover a range of research fields. Journal-level research categories are available only in SciVal and InCites. Although Dimensions and Lens.org employ these journal-level schemata as research area filters in their system, they apply these at the article level. This means that individual articles are being automatically reviewed through a machine learning algorithm and then a research area is applied regardless of the journal the article is published in.

ARTICLE-LEVEL RESEARCH CATEGORIES

Article-level research categories are research area classifications that have been assigned to an individual document. These classifications usually employ machine learning algorithms that create dynamic and ever-growing thesauri or a controlled list of topics that are assigned to the article and typically involve a much broader set of categories than the journal-level classifications. They differ from author-assigned keywords because the use of thesauri is meant to help standardize terms and reduce duplication or variants of the same concept. For example, they fix spelling variations—such as *floods*, *flooding*, and *flood*—by assigning a single term or phrase and will group similar topics based on citation linking or phrase analysis. All the bibliometric tools being reviewed in this section employ article-level classification using machine learning algorithms to match documents to topics.

SciVal's article-level classification has two hierarchical levels of classification, with new topics constantly emerging and being re-clustered using an in-house algorithm that is based on citation relationships. This approach allows for dynamic analysis and the identification of emerging research areas but poses issues with trend analyses and reporting reproducibility.

InCites' article-level classification has three hierarchical levels of classification, with most of the new topics and re-clustering happening at the lowest level. InCites uses an algorithm based on citation relationships developed by CWTS Leiden. The same analysis issues found in SciVal apply to InCites.

Lens.org's article-level classification does not have a clear hierarchical structure in the system; however, it uses OpenAlex as the data source, which does use a hierarchy for the concepts it defines. The OpenAlex algorithm uses the title and abstract of documents. Since the hierarchies are not available in Lens.org, the specificity of terms can vary greatly, causing more productive research areas to dominate the analysis when looking at large, broadly defined data sets.

Dimensions' article-level classification uses two different classifications, the Fields of Research (FOR) and the UN Sustainable Development Goals. The FOR uses a three-level hierarchy; however, it is not clear if the algorithm uses citation relationships or text-based analysis to determine the documents' category assignments. The UN Sustainable Development Goals does not have a hierarchy, and documents are matched to categories based on a combination of machine learning and keyword searches.

SOURCE TITLES

Source titles include any of the publication titles included in the data set. Normally, these include journal titles, conference proceedings, and so on. This is not only a standard entity type but also an essential entity type as most of the bibliometric analyses were born out of publication source analyses. One of the most important limitations to these systems is the titles' coverage of the data source. Each pulls in bibliographic data from different sources, as discussed in chapter 1, although there is some overlap with open data sources such as Medline, Crossref, and so on. Therefore, it is essential to report the source of the data set in any analysis for transparency on the limitations of the resulting bibliometric analysis.

The ability to look at the source titles by selected indicators allows evaluation for the purposes of collection development and publication decisions. All these systems allow source titles to be analyzed by subject area, output counts, citations, and other standard metrics. However, it appears that only Lens.org links patent citations to publication titles in its available analytics.

Table 2.3: Content type comparison between the major commercial bibliometric tools. Notes are included on funding/grant award amounts, patents, and news media.

	InCites	*SciVal*	*Dimensions*	*Lens.org*
Content Types				
Scholarly publications (articles, books, conference proceedings, etc.)	yes	yes	yes	yes
Usage data	no	yes	no	no
Funding/grant award amount[a]	no	yes	yes	no
Clinical trials	no	no	yes	no
Patents	yes[b]	yes[c]	yes[d]	yes[e]
Data sets	no	no	yes	yes
Policy documents	no	no	yes	no
News media	no	yes[f]	no	no

a. Although funding body data is captured at the article level in all these tools, only SciVal and Dimensions ingest data directly from the funding bodies to enable reporting on awarded amounts at the institution and country level.
b. Data sources: draws data from Clarivate-owned Derwent Innovation, including 59 patent office sources.
c. Data sources: European Patent Office, UK Intellectual Property Office, Japan Patent Office, US Patent and Trademark Office, World Intellectual Property Organization.
d. Data sources: European Patent Office, UK Intellectual Property Office, Japan Patent Office, US Patent and Trademark Office, World Intellectual Property Organization, German Patent and Trademark Office, Canadian Intellectual Property Office, Intellectual Property India, Intellectual Property Office (UK), National Industrial Property Institute, Intellectual Property Department (Hong Kong), Russian Patent Office.
e. Data sources: European Patent Office, US Patent and Trademark Office, Intellectual Property Australia, World Intellectual Property Organization.
f. New media sourced from LexisNexis Metabase (2013–) into Elsevier's Newsflo system.

FUNDING BODIES

Funding bodies data is derived from the bibliographic metadata, not through the funding source, and does not capture details about the amount awarded within the grants. Therefore, although funding bodies are an entity type that can be analyzed within all these bibliometric tools, only SciVal and Dimensions report the actual award amounts. This is because they ingest funding amounts directly from the funding bodies and connect this data with institution- and country-level data. See the document type "Funding/grant award amount" in table 2.3 for more details.

Funding body data and award data are of high interest to bibliometric tools as their user base expands to include research administrators and other university units interested in having a clearer link between awarded grants and their research impacts.

PATENTS

Patents are a challenging entity type to capture in bibliometric tools because they do not adhere to the common bibliographic standards, making them difficult to connect to research outputs. The most comprehensive patent data is available in Dimensions and Lens.org. This patent data makes these tools stand out from the other two systems as they provide detailed patent data that is separated out from the data available for scholarly publications and can therefore be searched and analyzed using unique fields such as inventor, owner, legal status, and so on.

Although InCites and SciVal do not have patents as a separate entity type for analysis, there are patent metrics, such as patent-citation counts, available in these tools. This is accomplished by linking documents to each other through shared metadata fields. For example, a research publication might be cited in a patent article, allowing these two separate documents to be connected. This would mean the article has received a patent citation. Analysis of articles containing patent citations can be accomplished in any of these tools by creating a publication set from either search results or the presented patent-citations bibliometric indicator in the system. Once the unique publication data set is created, any of the analysis options that are standard within the bibliometric tool (i.e., research areas, years, collaborations, and publication lists) are possible.

Bibliometric and Network Analysis Tools

Bibliometric and network analysis tools are likely to be considered the premier type of bibliometric analysis tools within the bibliometric (and scientometric) research community and with advanced level practitioners. They tend to be used for more in-depth bibliometric studies due to the additional technical training or knowledge that is required to use these applications. However, there is a spectrum among these tools—from the more user-friendly (VOSviewer, VOSviewer Online, Biblioshiny, CitNetExplorer) that do not require any programming knowledge, significant data cleaning, or training to the more advanced (Bibliometrix, CiteSpace, SciTools, SciMAT) that do require more advanced training and knowledge. This should not discourage the keen practitioner or scholar;

Table 2.4: List of the most commonly used bibliometric and network analysis tools

Product Name	Description	Owner/Developer
CitNetExplorer https://www.citnetexplorer.nl/	Bibliometric analysis with citation graphs (download)	CWTS Leiden University
Bibliometrix https://www.bibliometrix.org/home/	Bibliometric and network analysis package (download)	Bibliometrix
Biblioshiny https://www.bibliometrix.org/home/index.php/layout/biblioshiny	Bibliometric and network analysis software (online, no coding)	Bibliometrix
VOSviewer https://www.vosviewer.com/	Bibliometric network analysis software (download)	CWTS Leiden University
CiteSpace https://citespace.podia.com/	Bibliometric network analysis software (download)	Chaomei Chen
VOSviewer Online https://app.vosviewer.com/	Bibliometric network analysis software (online)	CWTS Leiden University
Sci2 Tool https://github.com/CIShell/sci2/releases/tag/v1.3.0	Bibliometric and network analysis software (download)	Indiana University and National Science Foundation
SciMAT https://sci2s.ugr.es/scimat/	Bibliometric and network analysis software (download)	University of Granada

Note: HistCite is not included here because it does not appear to be maintained. Although it can still be downloaded and used, more advanced and user-friendly options are available.

there are certainly many cases of bibliometric practitioners and other nonexperts who have been able to upskill very quickly. However, with this large spectrum of tools, nontechnical practitioners of bibliometrics can gain fairly quick entry to this class of tools, and scientometric researchers will find the advanced and statistical functions within these tools advantageous to their in-depth research questions.

Table 2.4 lists the main network analysis tools. There are some variances in the details of their functionality; however, all these tools have three main workflows:

1. **Data ingest and entity management:** The data set is imported using standard data files that have been created and exported from a bibliographic source. As discussed in chapter 1, these sources are typically Web of Science, Scopus, Crossref, and OpenAlex. The data files can be saved as raw files within the systems to allow for multiple analyses depending on the entity type. For example, authors, documents, countries, and institutions can be used as the main entity types.
2. **Select network analysis options:** There are several types of network analysis that these tools offer, including co-citation analysis (using authors, documents, or journals), keyword co-occurrence analysis, bibliographic coupling, coauthorship, and citations.
3. **Data visualization:** The mapping visualizations and access to the underlying data are the shining features of these tools. They apply advanced natural language processing, mapping algorithms, and in-system data cleaning (via thesauri, etc.) that make the clustering and mapping visualizations deceptively easy to create.

What Is Bibliometric Network Analysis?

A bibliometric network is a visual representation of the relationship between bibliographic objects. In technical terms the objects are *nodes* and the relationships are *edges*, represented by lines, and they can indicate not just the existence of a relationship but its strength as well. Bibliographic nodes, which are also referred to as entities in this report, are publications, journals, researchers, or keywords. The relationships (edges) studied can include co-citations (with authors or documents), keyword co-occurrence, bibliographic coupling, coauthorship, and citations, as were also previously mentioned (van Eck and Waltman 2014; Chen 2017).

CO-CITATION ANALYSIS

Co-citation analysis allows documents to be analyzed based on shared citing documents. This means that two documents will be linked because they have both been cited by the same document. The strength of the relationship between two documents is determined by the number of shared co-citing documents. Analysis of co-citations can be done with documents, authors, or journals as this main entity (or node).

BIBLIOGRAPHIC COUPLING

Bibliographic coupling also allows documents to be analyzed based on having shared citations in their

Table 2.5: List of additional bibliometric and network analysis tools currently available that are not detailed in table 2.4, as they are either not frequently updated, regionally specific, or less well-known

Product Name	Description	Owner/Developer
BibExcel https://homepage.univie.ac.at/juan.gorraiz/bibexcel/	Bibliometric analysis package (Excel)	Olle Persson
Scimeter https://scimeter.org/	Bibliometric analysis software (limited, arXiv.org source)	Frankfurt Institute for Advanced Studies
ScientoPy https://www.scientopy.com/en/	Bibliometric analysis software (limited, graphs)	University of Cauca
CRExplorer https://andreas-thor.github.io/cre/	Bibliometric analysis software (limited, historical citation analysis)	Andreas Thor, University of Applied Sciences for Telecommunications, Leipzig
RPYS i/o http://www.leydesdorff.net/comins/rpys/index.html	Bibliometric analysis software (limited, historical citation analysis)	Virginia Tech Applied Research Corporation
VIPER https://www.openaire.eu/viper-the-visual-project-explorer	Bibliometric and network analysis software (limited use)	OpenAire
Metaknowledge https://uwaterloo.ca/networks-lab/projects/metaknowledge	Bibliometric and network analysis software (limited use)	University of Waterloo
Scholarometer https://scholarometer.indiana.edu/	Bibliometric network analysis software (limited)	Center for Complex Networks and Systems Research, Indiana University Bloomington
Social Science Research Network (SSRN) https://www.ssrn.com/index.cfm/en/	Bibliometric ranking data	Elsevier (bought from Social Science Electronic Publishing Inc. in 2016)
Scimago Viz Tools https://www.scimagojr.com/viztools.php	Bibliometric visualization tool	Scimago

reference lists. This means that two documents will be linked because they have both cited the same document. Again, the strength of the relation between two documents is determined by the number of similar citations within their reference lists. Bibliographic coupling can be done with documents, journals, authors, institutions, or countries as the main entity (or node).

KEYWORD CO-OCCURRENCE

Keyword co-occurrence allows documents to be analyzed based on having shared keywords within their text, usually the title, abstracts, and listed indexed and author keywords. The strength of the relationship between two documents is determined by the number of shared keywords. The nodes presented in these analyses are the keywords themselves, and this approach is a popular analysis for looking at the clustering of research domains within a group of documents.

COAUTHORSHIP ANALYSIS

Coauthorship analysis allows documents to be analyzed based on having shared authors. Authors who frequently publish together therefore have stronger relationships. Coauthorship analysis can be done with individual authors, institutions, or countries. The relationships for institutions and countries are determined by the authorship; however, at these levels the data is aggregated to the institution or country level based on the affiliation information in the document's bibliographic information.

CITATION ANALYSIS

Citation analysis is one of the simplest analyses. It allows documents to be analyzed based on the number of times they cite one another. Although simple, this analysis tends to yield fewer relationships because of the direct relatedness needed between the documents (van Eck and Waltman 2014).

Other Bibliometric and Network Analysis Tools

Table 2.5 lists other bibliometric and network analysis tools that are currently available. These tools appear to be more limited in their scope of features, functionality, or adoption; however, they are still worthy of mention as many have been developed by researchers and research institutes that study and perform bibliometric network analyses as their field of research.

An Explosion of Discovery Tools

The landscape of bibliometric tools can be very confusing. This confusion is exacerbated by the recent

Table 2.6: Discovery tools using a variety of network analysis functions to aid users in research discovery

Product Name	Type of Tool
CiteSeerX https://citeseerx.ist.psu.edu/	Discovery
Scinapse https://www.scinapse.io/	Discovery and analytic consultancy
Open Research Knowledge Graph https://orkg.org/	Discovery and workflow management
Scilit https://app.scilit.net/	Discovery with analytical views
Google Scholar https://scholar.google.ca/	Discovery with analytics views
Academia.edu https://www.academia.edu/	Discovery with analytics views and author level impact
ResearchRabbit https://www.researchrabbit.ai/	Discovery with citation graphs
Connected Papers https://www.connectedpapers.com/	Discovery with citation graphs
Litmaps https://app.litmaps.com/	Discovery with citation graphs
Inciteful https://inciteful.xyz/	Discovery with citation graphs
PURE suggest https://fabian-beck.github.io/pure-suggest/	Discovery with citation graphs
CitationGecko https://www.citationgecko.com/	Discovery with citation graphs (no longer maintained)
CoCites https://www.cocites.com/	Discovery with citation graphs
Scite https://scite.ai/	Discovery with citation influence/contextualization and citation graphs
Semantic Scholar https://www.semanticscholar.org/	Discovery with citation maps and citation influence/contextualization
Open Knowledge Maps https://openknowledgemaps.org/	Discovery with keyword graphs
Yewno https://www.yewno.com/	Discovery with knowledge graphs
Iris.ai https://iris.ai/	Discovery with workflow management
Elicit https://elicit.org/	Discovery with workflow management
Scholarcy https://www.scholarcy.com/	Discovery with workflow management

explosion in the development of discovery tools that use bibliometric networks analysis as a method of research discovery (table 2.6). Many of these tools use a single seed or set of seed documents to present relevant research to the user. The idea is that the papers linked to these seed papers are highly relevant based on the co-citation, bibliographic coupling, or similar network mapping that they employ. The user can then navigate through the presented papers and select those that are of interest. Although these tools are very fascinating and are gaining popularity within the academic community, they are not useful for bibliometric analysis as the data is not presented for analysis but rather discovery, and therefore the systems do not often have adequate explanatory documentation for the user to understand and report the details of the methodology of analysis. Despite this, there is interest and evidence of these systems being used to supplement traditional search methods for systematic reviews, and they may become a standard method for reviews in the future.

There are also discovery tools that are beginning to contextualize the types of citations that are contained within research papers. They not only identify the existence of a citation but also make some assessment of the value of the citation to the original document. Scite and Semantic Scholar are two such research discovery tools that approach this challenge in different ways. Scite reports citations as "supporting," simply "mentioning," or "contrasting." Semantic Scholar reports the intent of the citations as either "background," "methods," or "results" and also indicates the velocity, acceleration, and whether the paper has influential citations. All these added features rely on the full text of the papers being available. Therefore, the data sources may be more limited than with the traditional bibliographic databases; this fact is a reason why these and similar systems are advocates for open access publishing options.

Choosing Tools That Are Right for Your Organization

Sugimoto and Larivière (2018) outline five key issues when considering bibliometric analysis that can also be applied when considering the tools that best fit the job at hand.

1. **Time:** Consider the constraints of publication and citation windows. First, quality scholarship does not happen quickly, and the accumulation of citations is known to take several years. Second, there are disciplinary differences in the life cycle of scholarship that need to be acknowledged and actions taken to mitigate unfair comparisons in any analysis.
2. **Data quality:** Data quality can be improved through data cleaning. Several bibliometric tools use unique identifiers for author names, institution names, funding bodies, and so on. Work can be done prior to analysis to improve the accuracy of this data. For example, ORCID is being adopted by many institutions as an open and nonproprietary author identification number. If the system uses ORCID, these numbers can be used to verify the identity of authors prior to analysis.
3. **Normalization:** When planning to benchmark across disciplines, the use of metrics that use normalization can help mitigate differences in data set size, disciplinary norms, and publication types.
4. **Coverage:** All bibliometrics data sets have limitations and constraints. It is important to be familiar with the content coverage of a data set. Research areas that are not adequately covered in the data set cannot be adequately analyzed.
5. **Alignment:** No analysis should be done without a clear objective. These are usually identified through clear research questions and the analysis, and selected metrics then must align with these questions. As discussed in chapter 1, the *SCOPE Framework* developed by the INORMS Research Evaluation Group (2020) provides more guidance on how bibliometric practitioners can align their analyses with the goal of using metrics responsibly.

When selecting bibliometric tools, consider these five factors. The tools you or your institution chooses will depend on your usage and what data you wish to analyze.

References

Chen, Chaomei. 2017. "Science Mapping: A Systematic Review of the Literature." *Journal of Data and Information Science* 2, no. 2: 1–40. https://doi.org/10.1515/jdis-2017-0006.

Guerrero-Bote, Vicente P., Zaida Chinchilla-Rodríguez, Abraham Mendoza, and Félix de Moya-Anegón. 2021. "Comparative Analysis of the Bibliographic Data Sources Dimensions and Scopus: An Approach at the Country and Institutional Levels." *Frontiers in Research Metrics and Analytics* 5 (January). https://doi.org/10.3389/frma.2020.593494.

INORMS Research Evaluation Group. 2020. *The SCOPE Framework: A Five-Stage Process for Evaluating Research Responsibly.* INORMS Research Evaluation Group. https://inorms.net/wp-content/uploads/2021/11/21655-scope-guide-v9-1636013361_cc-by.pdf.

Sugimoto, Cassidy R, and Vincent Larivière. 2018. *Measuring Research: What Everyone Needs to Know.* Oxford: Oxford University Press.

van Eck, Nees Jan, and Ludo Waltman. 2014. "Visualizing Bibliometric Networks." In *Measuring Scholarly Impact: Methods and Practice*, edited by Ying Ding, Ronald Rousseau, and Dietmar Wolfram, 285–320. Cham, Switzerland: Springer. https://doi.org/10.1007/978-3-319-10377-8_13.

Applications of Bibliometrics

This chapter is intended to inspire ideas for the practical use of the tools discussed in the previous chapter and to help practitioners connect information needs with the types of bibliometric analyses that might help respond to these needs. It is appropriate here to remind ourselves of the very important challenge of using metrics responsibly, as discussed in chapter 1. If you are unsure where to start, the guidance available from the SCOPE Framework (INORMS Research Evaluation Group 2020) challenges us to think first about the "value of the entity" that is being evaluated or measured before using any bibliometric analysis. Using the SCOPE Framework as a starting point reminds us to use bibliometric analysis only if it matches our values and to avoid the streetlight effect (Freedman 2010) of counting things only because they can be counted. The SCOPE Framework also presents a very helpful decision matrix to help identify the amount of risk or impact involved depending on the motivation for using the analysis and what entity level is being evaluated (figure 3.1).

Somewhat aligned with this risk matrix, the applications of bibliometrics that will be discussed here are broken up into four types:

- collections development,
- ranking validations,
- strategic planning and unit-level analyses, and
- research groups and individual analyses.

Of course, there are likely infinite ways to organize the different analysis types. However, these groupings will also loosely align with the various bibliometric services at academic libraries or institutions. In presenting the applications, an attempt has been made to generalize the data or these details so that they can be adjusted to unique situations; however, in some cases there are references to more descriptive materials. It is recommended that you pursue these for further guidance and detail. The step-by-step instructions cannot be captured here as these tools are constantly changing and evolving. The idea is to get a sense of the possible.

There are already some very excellent sources that define and describe bibliometric indicators. *Measuring Research: What Everyone Needs to Know* by Cassidy R. Sugimoto and Vincent Larivière (2018) is a particularly succinct, yet thorough, recent review of the main bibliometric indicators, their limitations, and considerations in interpreting the data. Somewhat more dated, yet still very relevant, is *Measure Academic Research: How to Undertake a Bibliometric Study* by Ana Andrés (2009), which divides the indicators into several groups: descriptive indicators, author production, journal productivity, collaborations, author citations, and journal citations. These sources and those provided in the reference list are excellent resources for understanding the breadth of indicators that could be used in any bibliometric study. This report is taking a more practical approach to the use of these indicators and attempts to describe the use of bibliometrics for specific service-oriented applications that a practitioner may encounter.

With a focus on the practitioner, this report also has to acknowledge that the full spectrum of bibliometric methodologies cannot possibly be covered.[1] Certainly, there are highly skilled expert-level practitioners and teams that have exceptional experience with a variety of complex analyses using tools and skills that go beyond the reach of this report, such as building and using data science methods with machine language algorithms or complex relational databases. Instead, this report focuses on the use of the bibliometric tools discussed in chapter 2, attempting to give the entry-level to mid-level practitioner some guidance on the various applications of these tools. However, keep in mind that most bibliometric practitioners will be required to develop some comfort with downloading

		Country	Institutional	Group	Individual
Analysis	To understand	Low impact	Low impact	Medium impact	Medium impact
Advocacy	To show off	Low impact	Low impact	Medium impact	Medium impact
Accountability	To monitor	Low impact	Medium impact	Medium impact	High impact
Acclaim	To benchmark	Medium impact	High impact	High impact	High impact
Adaptation	To incentivize	Medium impact	High impact	High impact	High impact
Allocation	To reward	High impact	High impact	High impact	High impact

Figure 3.1
SCOPE Framework decision matrix

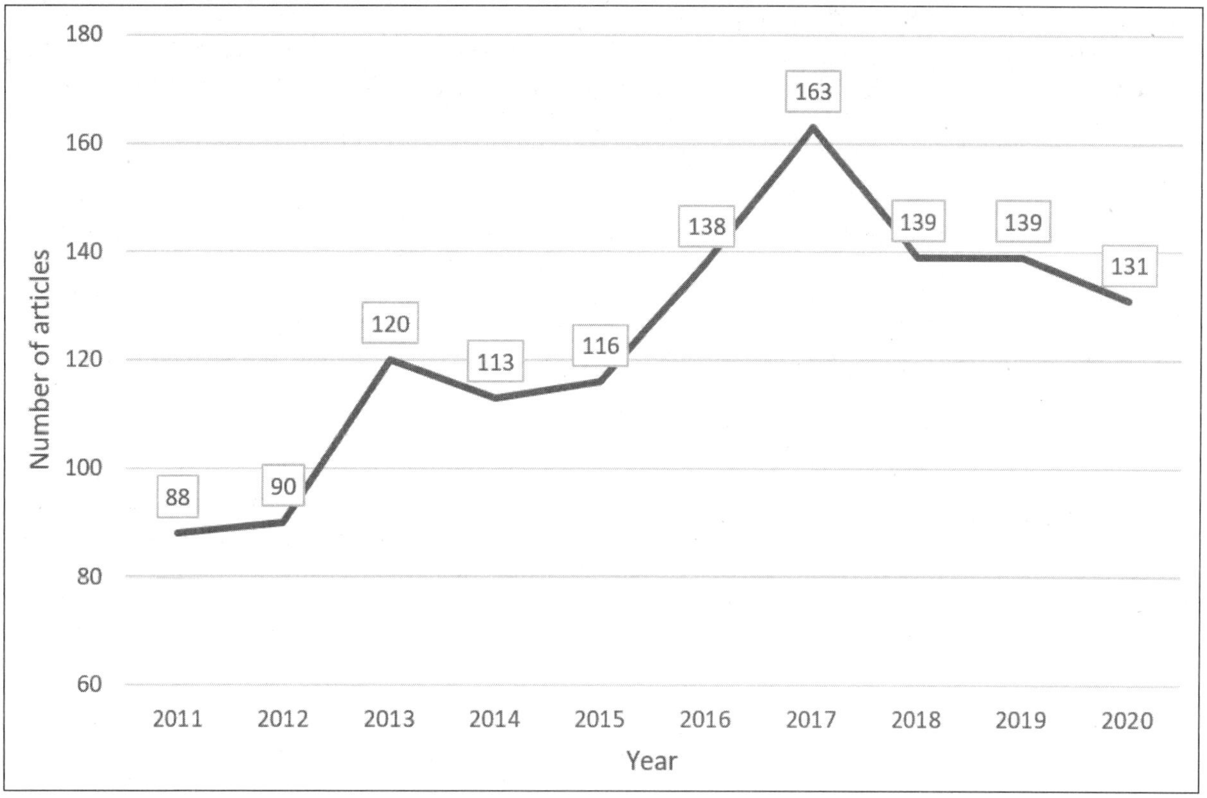

Figure 3.2
Number of University of Waterloo–affiliated journal articles from the publisher journal titles, 2011–2020. Total in this period is 1,237 journal articles.

and analysis external to the bibliometric tools. At the very least, developing a proficiency in using Excel pivot tables is certainly a good start.

Collections Development

Scenario 1: Looking at Potential Impact of a Transformative Agreement on Authors

A university library's collection development department wanted to know how many of its authors from its institution have published with a particular publisher in recent years to inform on the potential impact of a recent transformative agreement. Due to challenges in extracting complete publisher and journal data from some of the main bibliometric tools, the data source Crossref was used to create an API data pull using the affiliation name and publisher via its member code. With this analysis, the library was able to determine the count of affiliated articles published each year in journals by the publisher of interest, and the analysis would aid in year-over-year costing predictions if needed (figure 3.2).

Tools used: Crossref REST API and supporting documentation on GitHub.

Crossref REST API
http://api.crossref.org/

GitHub supporting documentation
https://github.com/CrossRef/rest-api-doc#resource components

Transformative agreements are shifting the way publishers and libraries do business. The not-for-profit Jisc represents the UK higher-ed sector as a consortium and negotiates deals on behalf of numerous member academic institutions. It has an interest in monitoring the impact of transformative agreements and recently presented at the Bibliometrics and Research Impact Community Conference on the methods used in its investigation (Harris 2022). In the presentation slides, there are several valuable resources it has created that may be of interest to the practitioner.

Jisc
https://www.jisc.ac.uk/

Scenario 2: Finding Core Journals Using Bibliometrics

Bibliometrics does not need to be complicated. When trying to understand collection development needs, bibliometrics can be used to tailor a core journal list to a particular research area, a group of researchers or author, an institution, or all of these together.

For example:

- A list of publications can be created using journal subject classifications or a tailored keyword search to define a research area and filter the results to your institution using a bibliographic data source such as Web of Science or Scopus. The resulting publication list can be uploaded into a bibliometric tool such as SciVal or InCites to analyze the journal or source list by several indicators such as total outputs, citation counts, or normalized indicators (table 3.1).
- The same publication list can be analyzed by citing and cited articles to get a list of journal titles (or other sources) related to the core publication list. This can help expand a core title list to include not just titles in which your authors are publishing but also titles they are using in the creation of their publications (table 3.2).
- The overlap between the title lists is highlighted with a gray screen in table 3.1 and table 3.2. Although this is just a simple example, it highlights that viewing the bibliometrics from different angles can help create a more robust picture of the resources that are valuable to a particular institution or research domain.

Scenario 3: Finding Core Journals Using Patent Literature

Galter Library at Northwestern University (Pastva et al. 2020) was interested in using patent literature to help identify highly cited journal publications within the health sciences research domain and to determine if these journals corresponded with usage within its existing collections (obtained from COUNTER usage statistics) and the Journal Impact Factor (obtained from InCites Journal Citation Reports). It used Dimensions as the bibliometric data source and was able to obtain NU author/inventor patent information as well as the journal article information that was cited within these patents. It found that the Journal Impact Factor did not correspond with the citation data or usage data and questioned its utility in making collection development decisions. However, the journal most cited in the patent literature did correspond with the usage data. From this analysis, Northwestern found that its existing collections aligned with the identified journals in its patent-citation analysis; however, a different set of top-cited journals, or core journals, were identified and could be used to help strengthen its collection development decisions. The visualization it used to help communicate these findings (although not reproducible here) plotted each journal along the *x*-axis in decreasing order of patent citation counts with secondary plots of the Journal Impact Factor and usage along the *y*-axis. Their work illustrates that patent citation has better alignment with usage counts versus the poor alignment with Journal Impact Factor.

Summary of tools: Dimensions (user interface and API), COUNTER, InCites, Excel, Python (and Jupyter), Tableau.

Further Reading on Bibliometrics for Collection Development

The following papers have not been referenced in this section, but they may be of interest to the reader.

Bangani, Siviwe, and Michiel Moll. 2021. "Scattering of Journals Cited in Legal Theses and Dissertations." *Journal of Librarianship and Information Science*, OnlineFirst, August 2021. https://doi.org/10.1177/09610006211036725.

Davis, Sarah, and Jan Thomas. 2020. "Bibliometrics in the Library: Beyond Research Evaluation." In "BibSymp20 Panel: Bibliometric Services 1." Panel presentation, Bibliometrics and Research Assessment Symposium 2020, online, October 7–9. YouTube video, 40:03–58:18. https://youtu.be/HbRBUDfkRWc?t=2403.

Table 3.1: Top 10 journal titles by scholarly output by affiliated author in the health technology research areas (defined by a keyword search). Titles shaded gray overlap with table 3.2. Data source: Scopus/SciVal.

Scopus Source	Scholarly Output	Views Count	Field-Weighted Citation Impact[a]	Citation Count
Lecture Notes in Computer Science	22	394	1.29	97
JMIR mHealth and uHealth	19	488	1.19	461
Progress in Biomedical Optics and Imaging—Proceedings of SPIE	14	203	4.24	51
Journal of Medical Internet Research	12	772	1.52	246
Scientific Reports	12	361	5.42	941
Sensors	9	296	1.34	141
PLoS ONE	8	311	4.47	521
ACS Applied Materials and Interfaces	6	257	1.8	182
Annual International Conference of the IEEE Engineering in Medicine and Biology—Proceedings	6	85	1.01	14
IEEE Access	6	100	1.89	132

a. The field-weighted citation impact (FWCI) is calculated based on the specific publication set being analyzed. Therefore, the value in table 3.1 will differ from the value in table 3.2 for a particular journal. The assumption is that the FWCI appears to be higher for all the titles in table 3.2 because of the tendency to cite already highly cited papers. These are therefore more likely to land in the reference lists of the affiliated authors.

Table 3.2: Top 10 journal titles by scholarly output referenced by affiliated author publications in the health technology research areas (defined by a keyword search). Titles shaded gray overlap with table 3.1. Data source: Scopus/SciVal.

Scopus Source	Scholarly Output	Views Count	Field-Weighted Citation Impact	Citation Count
Journal of Medical Internet Research	63	6,030	5.02	5,932
Scientific Reports	53	3,186	3.04	3,409
JMIR mHealth and uHealth	46	1,217	2.37	2,279
Lecture Notes in Computer Science	43	1,152	14.12	3,493
PLoS ONE	40	1,785	4.21	2,975
Sensors	35	1,847	2.72	1,887
ACS Applied Materials and Interfaces	33	2,015	3.27	2,243
Advanced Materials	27	3,186	8.51	5,011
IEEE Transactions on Neural Systems and Rehabilitation Engineering	24	1,295	2.42	967
The Lancet	24	28,804	457.41	86,331

Martindale, Tyler. 2020. "More Than Collection Development: Using Local Citation Analysis to Begin a Career in Business Librarianship." *Collection Management* 45, no. 4: 321–34. https://doi.org/10.1080/01462679.2020.1715315.

Pastva, Joelen, Jonathan Shank, Karen E. Gutzman, Madhuri Kaul, and Ramune K. Kubilius. 2018. "Capturing and Analyzing Publication, Citation, and Usage Data for Contextual Collection Development." *Serials Librarian* 74, no. 1–4: 102–10. https://doi.org/10.1080/0361526X.2018.1427996.

Stribling, Judy C., Matthew S. Robbins, and Antonio P. DeRosa. 2020. "Mapping the Literature of Guillain–Barre Syndrome to Support Current Awareness among Neurologists." *Journal of Hospital Librarianship* 20, no. 2: 111–19. https://doi.org/10.1080/15323269.2020.1738839.

Watwood, Carol L., and Terry Dean. 2019. "Mapping the Literature of Dental Hygiene: An Update." *Journal of the Medical Library Association* 107, no. 3: 374–83. https://doi.org/10.5195/jmla.2019.562.

Institutional Ranking Validation

The proliferation of university rankings has captured the attention of academic institutions around the globe, with administrative units contributing to the data submission and validation processes and including their ranking scores within university communications. It is now very common to see a ranking score on the splash page of a university website. However, rankings have been heavily criticized for reducing institutions to a few quantitative measures that mask significant nuance in the actual research and teaching missions of the institutions being evaluated (Gingras 2016). There is also a lack of consistency and transparency within and between the methodologies undertaken by the ranking bodies. Therefore, the rankings can seldom be compared from year to year and certainly cannot be compared to each other. Despite this, the participation in rankings is not slowing down. For example, since the introduction of the UN Sustainability Goals as an assessment benchmark within the Times Higher Education (THE) World University Ranking in 2019, there has been considerable uptake in the institutions participating, growing from 467 in 2019 to 1,410 in 2022. This increased attention to rankings means that the bibliometric indicators are also gaining greater attention as a result. Access to the methodologies is therefore important if institutions are going to be able to understand, keep up with, and maybe even push back on how they are being ranked. It is in the institutions' best interest to be able to understand and respond to changes in their rankings.

It is, however, important to understand the motivations behind rankings and the use of any indicator for that matter. As Yves Gingras (2016) discusses in his very on-point book titled *Bibliometrics and Research Evaluation: Uses and Abuses*, there are lessons to be learned from reviewing the impacts of national rankings such as the UK Research Evaluation Framework (REF); the bibliometrics-based university-funding formulas of Australia, Flanders, and Belgium; and the French grandes écoles (Gingras 2016). At best these rankings provide flimsy proxies for more time-consuming qualitative measures such as peer review or the nuanced pursuit of truth via academic rigor, and at worst the specific indicators chosen bias the outcomes toward preconceived notions of rank—for example, a focus on total outputs biases toward larger, better funded institutions, which can be clearly seen in the overrepresentation of privately funded American universities in many national and international rankings.

The major ranking organizations are ShanghaiRanking, also known as the Academic Ranking of World Universities (ARWU); the THE World University Ranking; the QS World University Ranking; and the Centre for Science and Technology Studies (CWTS) Leiden Ranking. For a more complete list the IREG maintains a list of international rankings (IREG Observatory, 2021). However, nationally significant rankings are not covered.

Validating the QS World University Ranking

Each year the QS requests that submitting institutions validate the data that is to be included in their ranking. The data that is shared with the institution for validation is a combination of institutionally submitted data and Scopus source data that QS extracts and analyzes. The bibliometric data includes gross number of papers, gross number of citations, net number of papers, normalized number of papers, net number of citations including self-citations, net number of citations excluding self-citations, and normalized number of citations. The details of the methodologies that QS applies to generate these values are detailed in its methods documentation. Although the methodology cannot be completely replicated, the data is based on institutionally affiliated documents within a specified five-year publication window. To obtain all the necessary bibliographic metadata for each article, the SciVal data set needs to be employed. This is because information such as the number of affiliations and the All Science Journal Classification scheme used in its methodology are not available directly from the Scopus data, and therefore the publication sets have to be pulled from SciVal. This validation set allows institutions to have some control over the data that is being used in the ranking and also provides an opportunity to learn more about the methodology, along with its strengths and weaknesses, and can inform the institutions on areas where they may see opportunities for growth or where they may prefer to remain less active.

> *QS Methods Documentation*
> https://support.qs.com/hc/en-gb/sections/360005689220-Methods

Validating the ShanghaiRanking

Even when the ranking organization does not involve the ranked institution in a data validation process, undergoing a data validation may still be of interest to the institution. For example, an institution might be interested in understanding what influenced a recent increase or decrease in its ranking in the ShanghaiRanking's global ranking of academic subjects. Using the methodology information provided by ShanghaiRanking, it could attempt to replicate the indicators used in the ranking, which include the number of journal publications with the Q1 Journal Impact Factor Quartile, the Category Normalized Citation Impact index value, the number of publications with international collaborations, and the number of publications that received the highest number of votes from the ShanghaiRanking Academic Excellence Survey. Keeping up to date with the institution's bibliometric indicators may aid in trend analysis or even identify high-performing research areas previously unidentified internally.

ShanghaiRanking Methodology
https://www.shanghairanking.com/methodology/gras/2022

ShanghaiRanking Academic Excellence Survey
https://www.shanghairanking.com/activities/aes

Strategic Planning and Unit Level Analyses

Bibliometrics can be more informative to institutions when they take a multidimensional approach to the data and break out of the confines of university rankings that reduce the complex organisms of academic institutions into a single rank-ordered list. Therefore, the analyses outlined here are only a jumping off point to give the reader some ideas of how bibliometrics can be applied when doing analysis for the purposes of planning at the university or strategic level. Using bibliometrics internally gives you more control over the data, and a more detailed story can be built. For example, in Canada the mostly public universities are funded partly based on the types of programs they offer, with medical schools not only being the best funded but also benefiting from a large network of affiliated hospitals and publishing in research areas that typically have high output and high citation rate. Therefore, universities without medical schools are certainly going to seem to underperform compared to these other universities. But not all universities can have medical schools. Therefore, it is important to make sure that the benchmarking is created in a way that is either comparing schools with similar characteristics or taking the differences into account. Otherwise, the bibliometric analyses will be hiding the real story behind a charade of misleading numbers.

Scenario 1: Benchmarking with National Comparators

An institution was interested in benchmarking against a set of its peer institutions in its country. However, this is entering a territory similar to ranking, where it is easy to reduce an institution to a rank using only a single (or at best a few) oversimplified indicators. As discussed above, benchmarking should be handled with great care. It is ideal to present a breadth of indicators or to use multidimensional analyses and ensure that the choices of comparator institutions, data filtering, and selected indicators are reasonable and clearly communicated. Therefore, the institution decided to use the SciVal data set, with

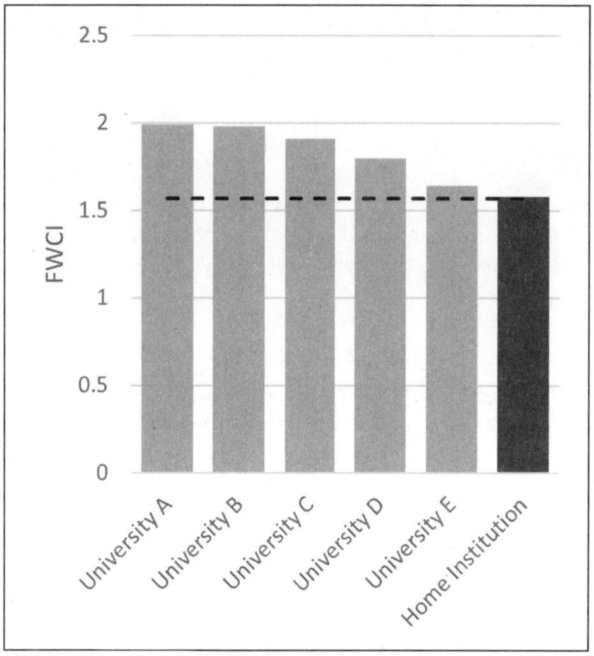

Figure 3.3
National comparison of FWCI, 2016–2020, with selected comparators, all subjects. Data source: Scopus/SciVal.

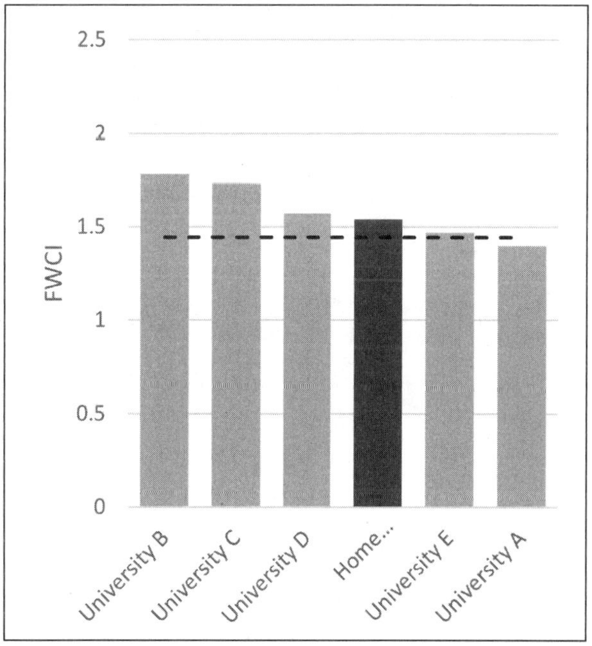

Figure 3.4
National comparison of FWCI, 2016–2020, with selected comparators, for non-medical science subjects. Data source: Scopus/SciVal.

the field-weighted citation impact (FWCI) as the main indicator, evaluate the data from a five-year window, and present the data in two figures, one including all subject classifications (figure 3.3) and another

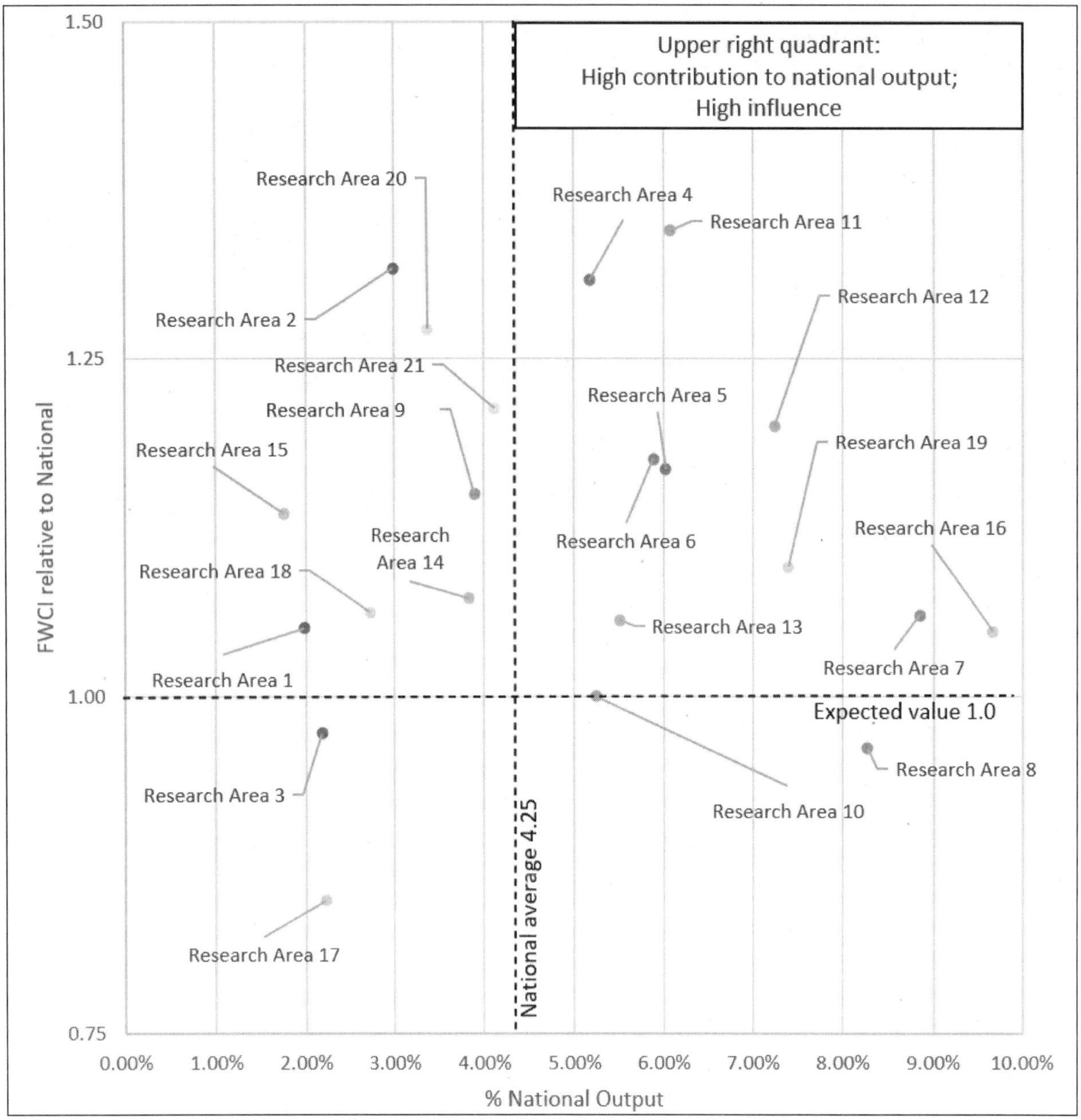

Figure 3.5
FWCI relative to the national average FWCI, plotted against the percentage of national outputs from the institution, by research area, 2016–2020. Source: SciVal.

that has publications from the medical sciences and related fields filtered out of the data (figure 3.4). This allowed the institution to clearly see the effects of having a medical school on even a normalized citation index like the FWCI and that there is obviously an advantage to focusing on the medical sciences. The message is not necessarily that the university should pursue a medical school or even more research within medical science. Rather, it is clear that the university has strengths outside of these research areas. What these strengths are precisely cannot be determined from this unidimensional analysis. Therefore, it may want to investigate further.

Tools used: SciVal and Excel.

Scenario 2: Understanding the Research Focus of an Institution in the National Context

Following the previous analysis, the institution was interested in understanding some more detail about the research areas that make it stand out at the national level. Therefore, it used a multidimensional approach that plotted its share of the national output and its FWCI for a series of journal-level research areas based on the All-Science Journal Classification (ASJC) from Scopus over a five-year period (figure 3.5). Quadrants were created using the national average output for all subjects and the expected FWCI of 1.00. The subjects that fall in the upper right quadrant are research areas that not only are above the national average but also have a higher impact (based the FWCI) than expected. This means that these are likely important research areas at this institution. But what about the research areas that have a high FWCI but a low share of the national output? Are these areas that are not of interest to the institution? It is hard to tell with this analysis, but there are some possible explanations: these research areas have a few highly impactful researchers who consistently maintain this level of impact, these research areas happen to have some outlier publications that have been particularly highly cited during this time frame, or the publications in these research areas also fall under more highly cited research areas and benefit from that association. These explanations are all conjecture, of course. The devil is in the details, and further investigation would help fill in the gaps in the story.

Tools used: SciVal, Excel

Scenario 3: Exploring the Effects of International Collaboration

The researchers Pablo García-Sánchez and Manuel J. Cobo (2018) wanted to explore the impact of international collaborations with the researchers from universities within the Andalusian region of Spain. They wanted to know if publications with more geographically diverse authorship collaborations would see higher citation rates. They used the Dimensions API and Python code to export publications from the nine public universities of Andalusia, identified using the Global Research Identifier Database. They filtered the publications to include only articles as the publication type and the publication years 2010–2015. They were interested in looking at papers authored by only one university in Andalusia, papers where all the authors belonged to Andalusian universities, papers where all the authors were Spanish and at least one was Andalusian, and finally all the Andalusian-authored papers with coauthors from any region of the world. This provided a very interesting perspective on collaboration networks and the progressive diffusion of authorship collaboration types. The papers in the group that had the most geographically diverse authorship collaborations were much more likely to receive a high number of citations. Further details of this study, including all the figures from the analysis, are available in the full paper (García-Sánchez and Cobo 2018). On the other hand, it must be kept in mind that confounding factors could affect the citations obtained by these authorship collaborations, such as the simple effect of more authors on a single paper meaning it may receive more citations. Controlling for these variables may be needed to get a clearer picture of the real impact of authorship collaborations.

Tools used: Dimensions, Python

Interdisciplinarity Analyses

The areas of interdisciplinarity analyses using bibliometrics are too complex to illustrate in a short example here. Therefore, we will explore the variety of methodologies outlined by Larivière and Gingras in their book chapter "Measuring Interdisciplinarity" (Larivière and Gingras 2014). They outline that interdisciplinarity has been measured in the following ways:

- identifying the authors' disciplinary affiliations using cited and citing references by either
    - measuring the percentage of citations made by sources outside the discipline or
    - measuring the percentage of papers from a group of researchers that publish papers outside their "main" discipline
- identifying articles that are published in journals classified in more than one research area, using standardized classifications such as the ASJC or Web of Science categories
- measuring the movement of a researcher from one discipline to another throughout their career

Research Group and Individual Analyses

Analyses at the research group or individual level require access to author-level data from a bibliometric data source. Although it is possible to create publication sets based on author name or author ID searches within any bibliometric tools or their associated data source, it is only SciVal that currently allows the creation and management of author groups and hierarchies within its system. This provides a great advantage to the system as groups can be created regardless of the accuracy of their affiliation information. For example, a researcher may forget a credit in a paper to a department where they are working as an adjunct faculty member. They may just fill in their main institution and department as their affiliation. However, the other institution may still like to count that paper in its analysis. It can do so by including the researcher in a group in SciVal. With this example in mind, this section illustrates two examples where the SciVal author tool provides an advantage for the analysis. However, similar analysis may be possible with the other bibliometric tools with a bit of creativity or by working through a few more steps, such as creating a search string of author IDs.

Scenario 1: Investigating the Impact of Mobility on Early-Career Researchers

The researchers Maxim Kotsemir, Ekaterina Dyachenko, and Alena Nefedova were interested in looking at the impact of mobility on young, early career researchers at the National Research University Higher School of Economics. Using the researchers' curricula vitae, they were able to select researchers based on their age (< 39 years) and sort them according to whether or not the researcher had past international educational opportunities that lasted at least three months. With this set of mobile and nonmobile researchers, they uploaded the researchers' Scopus author IDs into SciVal and organized them into their respective groups. This enabled them to analyze the two groups of researchers based on a number of bibliometric indicators, including number of publications, number of publications per researcher in each group, average number of citations per publication, and the field-weighted citation impact, among others. This study found that there was a positive correlation between mobility and a number of indicators such as number of papers, the prestige of the journal (based on the CiteScore), and citations (Kotsemir, Dyachenko, and Nefedova 2021).

Scenario 2: Exploring the Impact of Coauthorship on Citations

The researchers Nicola Cucari, Ilaria Tutore, Raffaella Montera, and Sofia Profita wanted to further analyze a list of top-cited authors in the field of corporate social responsibility that they discovered through a topic analysis in SciVal (Cucari et al. 2022). They were interested in understanding more about the collaboration activities of these authors based on the assumption that authors with more international collaborations do not always have higher publication output or citations.[2] They used the author identifier ORCID to create publication sets from the Scopus database that could be uploaded in the VOSviewer system for network analysis. The resulting visualization of the coauthorship analysis by countries illustrated the relative productivity of each country in the field of corporate social responsibility and how strongly connected each country was based on the number of coauthored papers. The strength of the connection was visualized by the closeness of the nodes (countries) and the thickness of the edges (number of coauthored papers). Their analysis showed that countries like the United States which have high productivity also have many coauthorship links; however, there are also countries like Australia with a good share of coauthorship links that are less productive . This may support the authors' assumption.

Tools used: SciVal, Scopus, VOSviewer

Notes

1. Only one example of a network analysis is used in the case studies presented in this report as many examples of scholarly research detail network analyses and comparatively few present case studies on the major commercial bibliometric tools. This report attempts to fill this gap. The paper by Makar and Trost (2018) provides some additional cases studies of network analyses that are directed at the practitioner.
2. Note that this contradicts the earlier example from García-Sánchez and Cobo (2018), who found that authors with more collaboration among external institutions had higher citations.

References

Andrés, Ana. 2009. *Measuring Academic Research: How to Undertake a Bibliometric Study.* Amsterdam, The Netherlands: Elsevier.

Cucari, Nicola, Ilaria Tutore, Raffaella Montera, and Sofia Profita. 2022. "A Bibliometric Performance Analysis of Publication Productivity in the Corporate Social Responsibility Field: Outcomes of SciVal Analytics." *Corporate Social Responsibility and Environmental Management*, online version of record. https://doi.org/10.1002/csr.2346.

Freedman, David H. 2010. *Wrong: Why Experts Keep Failing Us—and How to Know When Not to Trust Them.* New York: Little, Brown and Co.

García-Sánchez, Pablo, and Manuel J. Cobo. 2018. "Measuring the Impact of the International Relationships of the Andalusian Universities Using Dimensions Database." In *Intelligent Data Engineering and Automated Learning—IDEAL 2018: 19th International Conference, Madrid, Spain, November 21–23, 2018, Proceedings, Part II*, edited by Hujun Yin, David Camacho, Paulo Novais, and Antonio J. Tallón-Ballesteros, 138–144. Cham, Switzerland: Springer.

Gingras, Yves. 2016. *Bibliometrics and Research Evaluation: Uses and Abuses.* Cambridge, MA: MIT Press.

Harris, Beth. 2022. "Monitoring Transitional Agreements: The Challenges and Successes of Implementing Article Level Metadata Collection." Presentation at BRIC 2022: Bibliometrics and Research Impact Community Conference, Hamilton, ON, June 25–15, 2022. https://static1.squarespace.com/static/608c20ab643b700aeaad3d9f/t/62b4c824b0fdd44307d2c2da/1656014884570/bric-2022-Monitoring-TAs.pdf.

INORMS Research Evaluation Group. 2020. *The SCOPE Framework: A Five-Stage Process for Evaluating Research Responsibly.* INORMS Research Evaluation

Group. https://inorms.net/wp-content/uploads/2021/11/21655-scope-guide-v9-1636013361_cc-by.pdf.

IREG Observatory. 2021. “IREG Inventory on International Rankings.” https://ireg-observatory.org/en/initiatives/ireg-inventory-of-international-rankings/.

Kotsemir, Maxim, Ekaterina Dyachenko, and Alena Nefedova. 2021. “Publish More or Publish Differently? New Aspects of Relationship between Scientific Mobility and Performance of Young Researchers.” In *18th International Conference on Scientometrics and Informetrics, ISSI2021, 12–15 July 2021, KU Leuven, Belgium: Proceedings*, edited by Wolfgang Glänzel, Sarah Heeffer, Pei-Shan Chi, and Ronald Rousseau, 585–96. Leuven, Belgium: International Society for Scientometrics and Informetrics.

Larivière, Vincent, and Yves Gingras. 2014. “Measuring Interdisciplinarity.” In *Beyond Bibliometrics: Harnessing Multidimensional Indicators of Scholarly Impact*, edited by Blaise Cronin and Cassidy R. Sugimoto, 187–200. Cambridge, MA: MIT Press. https://doi.org/10.7551/mitpress/9445.001.0001.

Makar, Susan, and Amy Trost. 2018. “Operationalizing Bibliometrics as a Service in a Research Library.” *Information Outlook* (Online) 22, no. 5: 21–34.

Pastva, Joelen, Bart Davis, Karen Gutzman, Ramune Kubilius, and Aaron Sorensen. 2020. “Compelling Evidence: New Tools and Methods for Aligning Collections with the Research Mission.” *Serials Librarian* 78, no. 1–4: 219–27. https://doi.org/10.1080/0361526X.2020.1701393.

Sugimoto, Cassidy R, and Vincent Larivière. 2018. *Measuring Research: What Everyone Needs to Know.* Oxford: Oxford University Press.

Chapter 4

Bibliometric Service Models in Academia and Considerations Impacting Resourcing

All the information in this technical report is geared toward aiding bibliometric practitioners and their institutions to understand and select the right tools and technologies for their practice. In addition to understanding the technical aspects, choosing the right bibliometric tools for your institution will be heavily influenced by two important *strategic decisions*:

1. the type of services that are intended to be offered and
2. the expertise available.

Having a clear idea about the type of services, short-term and long-term, will influence the expertise that is required to provide these services, and this in turn will inform tool selection. This may seem like an obvious and simple idea; however, the challenge lies in choosing from the vast variety of services that fall under the bibliometric umbrella, some of which will be discussed further in this chapter. It is essential to recognize that nascent bibliometric services will rarely be able to offer a complete suite of services. Even when focusing on a smaller subset of services, a large array of expertise may be needed. Many experienced bibliometric practitioners will strongly advise that it is unrealistic to expect a broad range of services from a single individual or from a small team whose members are only partially dedicated to the service. Therefore, many successful bibliometric services often begin with small, focused objectives using existing expertise, with an eye for growth. For example, many libraries begin by using their existing liaison librarian model to support researchers in creating research impact profiles for individual researchers to support their grant applications or promotion and tenure packages, while other institutions may simply have an analyst, likely outside the library, providing some limited bibliometric analysis as part of a larger project monitoring research and other activities at the institutional level. In any case, it is essential to identify the intended service models and understand the expertise required to implement these services. Planning bibliometric service requires that careful, deliberate choices be made about the service capacity, as bibliometrics can take many forms, from focused, in-depth consultation-style analytical services to broadly scoped far-reaching services.

This chapter explores bibliometric services and how they may fit under the following service models:

- collaborative bibliometric services
- centralized bibliometric services in the library
- centralized bibliometric services outside of the library

We must also keep in mind that there are no professional standards set for bibliometric services, offering institutions ample flexibility for working outside these models and tailoring their services to local resources, expertise, institutional needs, and priorities. Some sage advice from a recent OCLC report on cross-campus partnerships within the research enterprise recommends approaching all research support services from a "social interoperability" perspective (Bryant, Dortmund, and Lavoie 2020). The report advises examining campus culture and stakeholder interests and employing intentional tactics to build relationships. Regardless of the service model employed, skilled relationship building is as important as the strategic decisions an institution makes around technical tools and personnel.

What Expertise Is Needed for Bibliometric Services?

It is probably impossible for a single individual to possess all of the expertise and offer the full spectrum of bibliometric services. Most likely, the institution has a limited service offering or has a team of individuals who provide their specialized skills to the bibliometric services. This may seem an obvious dichotomy of choice. However, when planning bibliometric services, careful, deliberate choices must be made about the service capacity given the spectrum of possible bibliometric services, from high-level strategically focused services to more in-depth concentrated analytical services.

Although there are no professional standards through certification or degree attainment, the "2021 Competencies Model for Bibliometric Work" (Lancho Barrantes, Vanhaverbeke, and Dobre 2021) underscores (1) the required knowledge in the field, (2) responsibilities and tasks, and (3) technical skills. Each area is subdivided into three levels: entry, advanced, and expert. The intention of these competencies, as stated in the documentation, is to identify skill gaps, to support progression through career stages, and to prepare job descriptions. Table 4.1 provides a summary of the skills covered in these competencies, and although we cannot cover all of these competencies here, they provide a very useful guide to planning and strategic decision-making around bibliometric services. Reviewing these competencies during planning and implementation stages of service building is highly recommended.

Table 4.1: Technical skills required for bibliometric work summarized from the "2021 Competencies Model for Bibliometric Work" (Lancho Barrantes, Vanhaverbeke, and Dobre 2021).

Skills	Details
Data use	download, clean, store, analyze, perform network analysis, visualize, interpret, compute bibliometric indicators
Tool use	data visualization software, statistical software, statistical programming packages, API use, AI packages
Scholarly communication	interactions of institutional repositories, research databases, preprint servers, persistent identifiers, bibliographic control

Bibliometric Service Models

The following models are being presented as representations and not as steadfast rules or an exhaustive review of the bibliometric services governance within academia. They are meant to be a guidepost for strategic decision-making, highlighting considerations for technical tools, expertise, and service levels. You may find your institution at an intersection between these models or providing services that do not quite fit under any of these models. However, the message here is that it is important to consider the impact of the model, whatever form it may take, that influences how decisions are made at your institution. You may find that some of the challenges you face are in fact entrenched in the structures at your institution, and overcoming them may mean considering alternative governance structures. These models are meant to help illustrate these possibilities.

Collaborative Bibliometric Services

In a collaborative bibliometric services model, institutions are likely to have the bibliometric work distributed across several service or administrative units. This model is characterized by (1) shared governance across these units or at least a strong interconnectedness through consultation and decision-making and (2) typically a focus on institutional level bibliometric analysis services motivated by strategic decision-making needs rather than supporting individual researchers for profile analysis. The engagement in collaborative bibliometric services across units is likely to grow out of a shared understanding of the value and impact that bibliometric services have within and outside of the individual units. This creates an environment where there is not only a shared understanding but also a shared commitment to and responsibility for the success of the services. Therefore, this creates more potential for shared resourcing through the use and selection of bibliometric tools and expertise. This model does not come without caveats. There is the risk of confusion around who actually provides the resources for tools and required expertise. There may also be the risk of territoriality, either by way of unclear delineations of responsibilities or by responsibility avoidance (Bryant 2022b). A collaborative bibliometric service model with its focus on institutional level analyses is likely to engage more strongly with units such as the university planning office or academic affairs and the research administration office.

EXEMPLAR: UNIVERSITY OF WATERLOO

The University of Waterloo is a PhD-granting, research-intensive Canadian university located in the city of Waterloo in the province of Ontario. It has developed collaborative bibliometric services through early engagement with several stakeholders across campus. As internal discussions at the university began to recognize a need for bibliometric services, a formal working group for bibliometrics was established by the vice-president academic and provost in 2013. Chaired by the associate vice-president research oversight and analysis, the working group currently engages core stakeholder units on campus including the library, institutional analysis and planning (IAP), and the office of research (OR). Additionally, members represent the other campus stakeholders, including the information systems and technology unit, academic units, and research centers and institutes. The working group provides high-level direction, advocacy, and guidance on the bibliometrics in response to campus needs. However, it does not function as a service provider. Instead, institutional level services are provided collaboratively by the core partners: the library, IAP, and OR. These units work very closely together to provide institutional level bibliometric analysis that emerges from needs such as ranking validations, strategic plan implementation performance insights, and support for grant applications. Even with close collaboration among these units, the library is a central partner in developing instruction, coordinating outreach, and supporting the distribution of bibliometric expertise across campus through training, instruction, and the coordination of its local community of practice. A full description of the bibliometric services at Waterloo can be found in the 2020 publication by Shannon Gordon and Alison Hitchens, *Library Impact Practice Brief: Supporting Bibliometric Data Needs at Academic Institutions* (Gordon and Hitchens 2020).

Centralized Bibliometric Services in the Library

Bibliometric services that are centralized within the library still often involve significant collaboration with units outside of the library. However, these collaborations are often not formalized through a shared governance structure. In North America, governance that is centralized within the library tends to take advantage of existing liaison librarians or specialized team-based structures. These services often initially focus on individual or departmental level supports and analysis and often structure services from a teaching and learning approach. This model is advantageous as these individuals can engage their existing relationships within the university and use existing core library skills, such as knowledge of scholarly publishing, research databases, and search methodologies. Arguably, linking levels of bibliometric analysis (e.g., individual vs. institutional) based on the governance model is a difficult distinction to make, as bibliometric services tend to diffuse through an institution as they gain traction. Therefore, a library with mature bibliometric services may very well have its services distributed throughout the institution. Certainly, as the bibliometric analysis skills within the library become better known across the institution, there are opportunities to identify shared values and priorities with other units. However, the bibliometric services that are primarily governed by the library will likely continually face familiar challenges such as repeatedly proving the value of the services to the broader institution and clarifying ownership of resources, decision-making, and tasks.

EXEMPLAR: SYRACUSE UNIVERSITY

Syracuse University is an R1 research university located in the city of Syracuse in the state of New York, USA. It has developed a bibliometric service model that is centralized within the library with close connections to other service units such as the office of research. The library has developed a research impact team that focuses its services on engaging in discussions related to responsible use of metrics, supporting outreach and education on the use of core bibliometric resources such as Scopus, Web of Science, Dimensions, and Lens.org, and supporting campus partners through the creation of reports using bibliometric analyses. It also leans on its existing liaison librarians to aid with information dissemination and relationship building within the academic units. With this model, Syracuse is a strong example of how libraries facilitate the diffusion of bibliometrics across a campus. Its bibliometric services are still relatively new, being undertaken in 2020, and its service model will likely continue to evolve as it establishes stronger connections across campus and builds expertise within and outside of the library.

A fuller description of the Syracuse model can be found in the OCLC *Hanging Together* blog post by Rebecca Bryant, "Establishing a Bibliometrics and Research Impact Team at Syracuse" (Bryant 2022a).

EXEMPLAR: UNIVERSITY OF NEW SOUTH WALES

By 2009, at the research-focused University of New South Wales, Sydney, Australia, a seven-member service team was developed from existing library staff. These individuals had their portfolios adjusted to allow at least 50 percent of their role to be committed to their Research Impact Measurement Services (what they locally call their RIMS) (Drummond and Wartho, 2009). They provided services mainly to individual researchers, schools, and faculties. Their primary function was to respond to requests and develop reports that included research impact analytics. These reports included grant application statements, research impact statements, citation counts, h-index scores, research trend reports, journal impact reports, and publication activity reports (Drummond and Wartho 2009).

THE EUROPEAN CONTEXT

Bibliometric services in the European context are considerably more mature than in North America.

An exemplar from Europe is the University of Vienna Library, which has a well-established bibliometric service. Its services are supported through a dedicated department for bibliometrics and publication strategies that has seven dedicated staff who provide bibliometric analysis from the researcher level through the institutional level. The department is also the administrative arm of the prominent European Scientometric Summer School (ESSS; https://esss.info/about/), which is a multi-institutional collaboration that provides training in bibliometric analysis to students, researchers, and practitioners.

In Europe, there are also more established academic research units that are dedicated to scientometrics. Among them are some internationally recognized units with which many bibliometric practitioners will be familiar, such as the Centre for Science and Technology Studies (CWTS) at Leiden University, the Netherlands; the EC3 Research Group at the University of Granada, Spain; and the German Centre for Higher Education Research and Science Studies (DZHW). The combination of these service- and research-oriented units has made Europe a noteworthy leader in the bibliometric community from which we in North America can learn and grow.

Centre for Science and Technology Studies
https://www.cwts.nl/about-cwts

EC3 Research Group
https://ec3-research.com/

German Centre for Higher Education Research and Science Studies
https://www.dzhw.eu/en/gmbh/index_html

Centralized Bibliometric Services outside the Library

Bibliometric services that are centralized outside the library are considerably more difficult to characterize as they are not as well known among the library community and are often part of internally reporting units without publicly available profiles detailing their services. Regardless, some basic characteristics have been summarized through reviewing roles across several institutions such as the Ohio State University (Strategic and Competitive Intelligence Office 2022), the University of Michigan Medical School (Office of Research 2022), Western University (Western Research 2022), and the University of Toronto (2022). Many of these universities have individuals outside of the library who are skilled in bibliometric analysis or who have access to and administer bibliometric tools. Their roles tend to be within units that are highly interested in tracking the outputs and impacts of research, such as the research administration office, president's office, or planning office. Additionally, stand-alone advisory units such as research intelligence offices appear to be becoming more engaged in providing highly tailored bibliometrics to the university administration. These units will likely experience similar service silos as those bibliometric services that are centralized within the library. However, they tend to be more reactive to specific operational goals, such as increasing funding in a specific research area, increasing the university's performance in international rankings, or taking part in a larger industry integration or business intelligence service.

Another interesting structure is the CWTS B.V., which is a company owned by Leiden University that offers research analytic services as a business. With its close affiliation with the Leiden Ranking and CWTS, this is an exceptionally interesting setup as it bridges both academia and commercial services. Although this is not a particularly plausible model for many institutions, it illustrates that bibliometric services can also be structured as a contractual service or consultancy. This type of service is also offered as a sort of boutique, for hire consultancy service from many of the companies that provide bibliometric data and tools.

This chapter does not supply an exemplar here as there is only limited information on this model and the services and structures vary so greatly among institutions that selecting a single exemplar would likely be misleading. Readers should explore the institutions cited in this section to find out more about their individual services and governance structures.

Conclusion

This chapter covers three main service models for bibliometrics at academic institutions: collaborative bibliometric services, centralized bibliometric services within the library, and centralized bibliometric services outside the library. It makes clear that any of these models and the mix of services that are possible will see success at your institution, emphasizing the value that bibliometric services have at the academy. There appears to be a progression in the user focus of the bibliometric services that is connected to the type of service models. With much more focus on individual-level services, such as supporting faculty in promotion and tenure applications or creating asynchronous learning objects, libraries first take the lead on bibliometric services. As the services begin to mature, connections are formed within other units and the services tend to broaden. Of course, this is a general observation and may not be the experience at every institution. However, there is a clear need to prioritize creating collaborative partnerships across an institution in any bibliometric work, regardless of the governance structure. Whether these connections are created through formal governance models or evolve through other channels, these partnerships will need to establish sustainable relationships that are not dependent on any single individual but are baked into the way the collaborating units interact around their bibliometric services.

The progression of bibliometric services will also impact the bibliometric tools that are used at the institution. Therefore, it is hoped that this chapter aids readers to reflect on the bibliometric tools presented in previous chapters and to begin to connect how their service models may impact the tools that will be most beneficial to their services now and how this may evolve in the future.

References

Bryant, Rebecca. 2022a. "Establishing a Bibliometrics and Research Impact Team at Syracuse University." *Hanging Together* (blog), February 18. https://hangingtogether.org/establishing-a-bibliometrics-and-research-impact-team-at-syracuse-university/.

———. 2022b. "Insights from a Recent RLP Discussion of Bibliometrics and Research Impact (BRI) Services." *Hanging Together* (blog), August 3. https://hangingtogether.org/insights-from-a-recent-rlp-discussion-on-bibliometrics-and-research-impact-bri-services/.

Bryant, Rebecca, Annette Dortmund, and Brian Lavoie. 2020. *Social Interoperability in Research Support: Cross-Campus Partnerships and the University Research Enterprise*. Dublin, OH: OCLC Research. https://doi.org/10.25333/wyrd-n586.

Drummond, Robyn, and Richard Wartho. 2009. "RIMS: The Research Impact Measurement Service at the University of New South Wales." *Australian Academic and Research Libraries* 40, no. 2 (June): 76–87. https://doi.org/10.1080/00048623.2016.1253427.

Gordon, Shannon, and Alison Hitchens. 2020. *Library Impact Practice Brief: Supporting Bibliometric Data Needs at Academic Institutions*. Washington, DC: Association of Research Libraries, October 28. https://doi.org/10.29242/brief.waterloo2020.

Lancho Barrantes, Barbara S., Hannelore Vanhaverbeke, and Silvia Dobre. 2021. "Competencies Model for Bibliometric Work," ver. 1.2. June. https://thebibliomagician.files.wordpress.com/2021/07/competenciesmodel_june2021-2.pdf.

Office of Research. 2022. "Research Intelligence and Analytics." University of Michigan Medical School. Accessed October 10. https://research.medicine.umich.edu/our-units/research-intelligence-analytics.

Strategic and Competitive Intelligence Office. 2022. "What We Do." Ohio State University. Accessed October 10. https://u.osu.edu/businessintelligence/.

University of Toronto. 2022. "Research Data and Analytics." Accessed October 10. https://research.utoronto.ca/research-data-analytics/research-data-analytics.

Western Research. 2022. "Knowledge Exchange and Impact." Western University. Accessed October 10. https://uwo.ca/research/services/kex/index.html.

Library Technology REPORTS

A Note to Our Readers

Library Technology Reports, which has been in print for fifty-eight years, ceases publication with this November/December 2022 issue (Volume 58, no. 8). We want to thank you for reading and engaging with us over the past five decades and for coming back for the latest updates in the library technology industry.

We also want to thank all the contributors over the years for sharing their expertise, tips, and thoughtful analyses with our readers. Their words have connected and inspired readers and colleagues in the field to enhance their technological knowledge and tackle new projects. We've seen issues covering everything from cloud services, online reference, and 3-D printers to data privacy, coding, and web accessibility.

As we, the staff members in ALA TechSource and ALA Editions, look forward beyond this final edition of *Library Technology Reports*, our intention is to continue providing content that inspires library workers to make informed decisions about their services, programs, and technology. We will continue to provide ongoing resources for the library field with professional development titles in a range of subjects—from intellectual freedom and copyright to programs and services. Our latest resources are available at www.alastore.ala.org.

If you have questions about your subscription, please contact us at subscriptions@ala.org or call toll free at (800) 545-2433, ext. 4299.

Thank you for reading!
—Samantha Kundert, managing editor, and the staff from ALA TechSource

ALA TechSource

alatechsource.org

ALA TechSource, a unit of the publishing department of the American Library Association

Notes

Notes

Notes